LE LIVRE DE

Promethea

THE BOOK OF

Promethea

HÉLÈNE CIXOUS

Translated &
with an introduction
by Betsy Wing

University of Nebraska
PRESS
Lincoln and London

Originally published as *Le Livre de
Promethea*, © Éditions Gallimard, 1983

Library of Congress
Cataloging in Publication Data
Cixous, Hélène, 1937-
[Livre de Promethea. English]
The book of Promethea –
Le livre de Promethea / by Hélène
Cixous; translated and with
an introduction by Betsy Wing.
p. cm. – (European
women writers series) Trans-
lation of: Le livre de Promethea.
Includes bibliographic references.
ISBN 0-8032-1443-X (cl : alk.)
ISBN 0-8032-6343-0 (pbk.)
I. Title. II. Series.
PQ2663.I9L5813   1991   843'.914 – dc20
90-41111   CIP
Second printing: 1996

A Translator's Imaginary Choices

Hélène Cixous was born in Oran, Algeria, in 1937. Today she is a professor of English literature at the experimental University of Paris-VIII-Vincennes, which she helped to found and which, through the vagaries of politics is no longer at Vincennes but at St.-Denis, a suburb of Paris. She is best known in the English-speaking world for her contributions to feminist theory, specifically her attempts to locate the underlying structures governing language and society that contain women in a position of passivity, and her formulations of a feminine libidinal economy as the positive force to achieving freedom from those constraints. But, as Verena Conley points out in *Hélène Cixous: Writing the Feminine,* she has never proceeded on a purely conceptual level. The writing of poetic texts has been one of the most important ways in which she has worked on displacing the limits imposed by Western society. She has been an extraordinarily prolific writer, and, since 1969, has produced more than twenty "fictional" works in addition to book-length essays and works for the theater.

Much of Cixous's work has been concerned with love and how it may be lived without one member of the couple (or both—though in our culture, most frequently the woman) being destroyed through a passive incorporation into the other. *The Book of Promethea* explores the risks that must be taken to be in love, that is, to know at every moment not just that one loves, but also that one is beloved. Because this is, for Hélène Cixous, a life-or-death situation, all of life's intensity is focused into these instants. They may be the moments of our everyday banal existence, but they acquire the power of all that we have seen and known, all our myths and history, all our moral torment, all our spiritual and physical pleasures.

Between life and the Cixousian text there lies only an osmotic moment, a present of writing or reading, in which everything is held very briefly in a living balance. For Cixous all writing is necessarily both autobiographical and fictional, shaped by history and the unconscious.

The pleasures and problems of translating Cixous begin, of course, with the very notions "author" and "translator." Along with Roland Barthes and Jacques Derrida, Cixous sees writing as a generous and generating process that escapes the control of its originator. From her earliest texts, she has been concerned with producing a work that gives the reader the desire to write, to enter into the process of desire that will permit the emergence of a certain sort of work. Speaking of this process she describes a "love story with dreams" where her part is to note down what emerges from her unconscious in an attempt to work with the forces that drive and pressure her, Cixous as I, the author. These forces then, become part of "writing," defined as a constant process of the production of meaning in which the reader is to participate as actively as the "original" writer. Although translation at its most seductive can feel as if one is letting words come in the eyes and out the fingers, or, as Cixous here describes her own writing: like a cardiograph—left hand on the body, right hand on the page (53) there is a lot of work that takes place somewhere between eyes and fingers. Despite their oneiric quality, Cixous's texts are not at all "automatic writing"; they consciously pose questions and give answers. The freedoms they offer a reader or a translator result from the demands they make.

One question that always arises (Cixous asks it of herself, the texts ask it of the readers, and politically conscious women ask it of Cixous, her texts, and her readers): are the poetic and the political not irreconcilable? As a writer who is deeply concerned with the position of women in society, Cixous can only answer no. She sees her work as one of reparation, not separation, and in an interview with Verena Conley she consolidated these oppositions in a chiasm: "poetically political, politically poetic."[1] For her, social structures are inextricably linked to the structures of language and she does not accept the possibility that theory and practice can be separate. She writes poetic texts that constitute a poetic praxis whose activity is to assure that women's voices will no longer be treated dismissively but will draw power from their experience of arbitrary, hypercoded language constructions. She sees the body, more or less feminine or masculine, as "always ciphered." Anatomy, incapable of commanding structures, is always already in language, which in every one of her texts engages in a dialectic with the physical.

Cixous defines this poetic praxis not in opposition to prose but as the bearer of a certain psychic density capable of subverting the ordinary codes of our perception. She both seeks out cliché to displace it—to repeat it as something different—and insists on a more powerful, conscious inhabiting of our cultural commonplaces. In particular, Cixous will pick up on the concepts of femininity that have kept women "in their place" in society and blow them up—as arbitrarily as they were imposed—to levels of power and exorbitance at which they can no longer be ignored.

A close reader of her texts can sense, accompanying the feminine libidinal effects that seem so effortless in her writing, her strong, intelligent consciousness of what she is doing. This consciousness and this doing—this subject—however, are removed from the notion of agency common to English and American philosophical tradition. Rather than agency the basis of the subject is a place, the active moment, at which these libidinal effects and a consciousness of them are produced—not unlike those places in the text where she will use a noun to function as a verb. Cixous calls this practice "writing from the body." Occasionally, judged in a reiteration of our Anglo-American tradition with its own system of clichés, one will hear it called "sentimental" or "self-indulgent." These clichés define feminine perceptions, states, and activities dismissively, in language that is supposed to be neutral. Neither for Cixous nor for her critics, however, can there be such a thing as neutral language—there is only language carrying and enforcing our deepest, earliest constructions and our unconscious participations in ideology.

It is precisely the clash between the neutralizing properties of cliché and the powerful hold it exerts over us and Cixous's intervention in this process that makes her writing subversive. And it poses particular problems of translation. Sometimes the cliché is cited and sited, one knows one is not dealing with a cliché cliché. Is this a function of the whole text? Or is there a marker there in the cliché itself? How can it be both a cliché and not a cliché? Is it at all possible to render this uneasiness, this question, in English?

And sometimes we are invited fully to inhabit a commonplace: a Common Place where a shared social basis, an agreed sense of existence is communicated—the very opposite of the platitudes necessary to describe it. The blood-mother-sea connection, for instance, where metaphor becomes literal and we are invited to swim, or the cave-bosom-womb she dares us to enter.

Connected with the problem of cliché is another. A major risk for a translator is the tendency to make a text so "readable"—so "natural"—in English that the words are effectively domesticated and, entering a realm of banality that is frequently the one Cixous seeks to displace, lose the psychic density essential to a poetic text. Derrida has suggested that "a 'good' translation must always commit abuses."[2] It must permit the text to escape the world of the usual, the world of common usage in translation. It must continue "seeking the unthought or unthinkable in the unsaid or unsayable."[3] The conflation of differences that I will refer to later is one small example of this basically cumulative technique.

This leads directly to Voice: the next important problem, as well as the greatest pleasure, in translating Cixous. Her texts are in many ways texts for the ear. She tries to write "with her eyes closed."[4] One of the means she uses to subvert everyday, useful language is to play with its surface music, in a Joycean confusion of phonic elements, calling our attention to what is encoded there and how we use it—which also at times implicates the visual with the phonic. (This is, of course, frequently untranslatable, as in "L'une" [this one] and *lune* [moon]). Voice, undefinable but much talked about, is probably the most important element both in terms of Cixous's theory of writing from the body and in terms of the pleasure of her texts in French. Voice, it seems to me, is best located and transmitted with closely literal translation: one which flaunts the clearly poetic quality of her texts—and yet takes poetic license to reproduce Cixousian wordplay and repetitions where they can appear easily and letting them slip away where they would be obtrusive and forced in English.

This privileging of voice comes from a number of different directions. On the deepest level, voice is linked with the mother in what Jacques Lacan refers to as the Imaginary stage. The child who has not yet learned she is not coextensive with the mother's body, as she first loses the coherence of enveloping liquid and sound, must experience her earliest sense of otherness by losing the sounds of her mother's body, and hearing the familiar timbre of her mother's voice come from another place. This is an intrinsic part of our coming into separate existence, preceding the famous mirror stage, in which the child comes to know of herself as a separate being by fixing the image of the people she sees around her on herself and identifying with their reflection of her. Voice comes from a moment beyond the alienation of culture, it is heard before there is an "I" to listen to it.

Voice has its rhythms, but it is hard to know and formulate what they are. They are not identical with the rhythms of breath or a beating heart. They intimate meaning. If breath stops, if a heart stops beating, death occurs. The rhythms of voice are connected to a body; they share in but are not the same as the universal tickings of this body. If voice stops, there is silence to listen to and the silence participates somehow in the same rhythm and the same intimate meaning. Connected to histories, cultures, and particular lives, voices, silences, and their meanings can never be quite the same universally, but they seem to invite us to inhabit some common place. This reoralization of language, remarked by Michel Benamou in his work on marginal literature, serves, as he says, "to reinstate the body in poetics (from which it has been absent since Aristotle.)"[5] And the common place it discovers is a unification with the human past back to the late Paleolithic—the time of Lascaux, the time flowing in and out of the present of *The Book of Promethea*.

Voice offers us something very specific, an odd cross between the deepest illusion and the deepest promise. The connection of its rhythms with body and specifically with the body of the mother is capable of drawing us in like music, lulling us, sucking us into a sense of existing in a moment of space and time in which we seem connected to another meaningfully and without mediation. This could be called a "fiction of presence"—an illusory offer of authenticity.

Cixous, however, in *The Book of Promethea* is working to repair the separation between fiction and presence, trying to chronicle a very-present love without destroying it in the writing. And she works with the promise of voice, which is quite specifically not the voice of a speaking subject, but voice that offers escape from the unity of self. Conflation of seemingly separate fields, such as fiction and authenticity, fiction and biography, sexte/texte, person and place, person and person, subject and object, is a technique that she has frequently used to provide escape from our coded perceptions of what is "natural."

And here is the conflict. Voice must be full of life. It must not participate in banal codes that destroy this life. Although we know that a "natural" voice is ideologically determined, the voice of the text must sound "natural" in some ways; it cannot sound like a strictly intellectual imposition on this language; which means it must use contemporary idiom—but not to the point of what we call cliché—at the same time that it locates the liveliest points of the text. These points have been called "clusters of textual energy" because they have forced some new meaning into being.[6] This process will be violent in the original language and the translator must recreate this violence. Because of the difference between relationships to language, it may be impossible to recreate the same violence in the identical position in the text. The French, for example (let us at least take pleasure in our commonplaces!), have always liked the little shiver of delight—the "frisson"—they feel when wrestling with ideas, whereas Americans seem happier smashing them. It is, however, necessary to do the same work as much as possible in the "target" language. A sense of what has taken place in the language of the original must enter into the new text. One of Cixous's techniques, here conflation of differences—in this case the difference between place and person, noun and verb, can be seen in the following example:

Quand? surtout à la maladroite et tâtonnante fondation d'une cité fragile, provisoire, tirée vive, mais toute tremblante de timidité, de ma terre imaginaire, surtout à la fondation de cette contrée incertaine, cette chose, cette folle créature, ce mirage plus fort que moi, cette enfant incontrôlable, qui m'obéit et me désobéit, vient de moi et s'en va de moi, et à peine partie de moi, m'échappe, s'élève, montagne, galope, et je dois aussitôt me mettre à gravir, à chevaucher, je dois tenter de la rattraper, mais je ne dois pas me faire d'illusion: à peine surgie, elle est loin, moi l'archère, elle la flèche. (*Le Livre de Promethea*, p. 16)

[When? . . .especially at the groping, clumsy beginnings of a fragile, temporary city, pulled alive but shivering all over with shyness, out of my imaginary earth. Especially at the beginnings of this doubtful region, this thing, this crazy creature, this mirage that is stronger than I, this uncontrollable child, who obeys and disobeys me, comes from me and leaves me, and who scarcely having left, gets away, rises, mountain, gallops, and immediately I have to start climbing, straddling, I have to try to catch her. But no wishful thinking: she is barely up and already far away, I the archer, she the arrow.] (p. 9)

We see her canceling the barrier between acting subject, object, and action. Cixous does not say "gallops over a mountain," "rises like a mountain," or "is a mountain," but rather sets the noun *montagne* in a series of verbs where phonically it seems to function exactly like a verb. I did not add the *s* that would make it into a verb in English, because there is no such marker in French. My hope is that the echo with the colloquial "mountin"—as in "mountin' a horse"—works to make it a verb, as, perhaps the final *e* on *montagne* seems to link it to *galope* (whose noun is *galop*).

Cixous's incorporation of myth and of other texts in her work can be seen to function in much the same way as her use of cliché. Though she quotes and displaces these, she also identifies herself with them, taking them as another instance of our cultural commonplaces. *La Saison en enfer* (A Season in Hell) by Arthur Rimbaud suddenly coincides with *The Arabian Nights* as Cixous depicts the eternity of the living and loving moment, its sudden flash and the pleasure in spinning it out in her Season in Paradise. Her use of other "author's" texts, while sounding problematic, is the least of the problems posed for translation. It merely dares and invites yet another version. One of the glorious moments in translating *The Newly Born Woman* was the pleasure in turning a French Shakespeare into Shakespearean, Cixousian, contemporary, American English. And it is one of the most translatable instances of the conflation of life/fiction/sexte/texte.

Myth, on the other hand, requires that that other hand have a delicate touch. It is like cliché, except it marks itself—with the names of characters and recognizable events—at least for the generations (passing now, perhaps?) whose cultural grounding includes Greek heroes and the Old Testament's struggles with God and His Law. Cixous uses myth to bring the ordinariness of daily life into the level of expression perceived as the realm of our most universal struggles and longings. She once again insists on making what is normally deprecated (that is, treasured for its small charms) into the extraordinary, the extravagant.

It is extremely difficult to make these myths move from their position as citation, where they can fluctuate obstinately between the jaded and the strange. They never do seem "natural." And that is part of the point. As citations they re-mark our culture. As changed citations (as in the feminization of the name Promethea) they are no longer schoolbook recitations but projections of Cixous's desires into culture. The magical identification of inscription with an effect in reality, so powerfully visible in the drawings at Lascaux is one of Cixous's aims in chronicling the present event of love. Like the incorporation of the cave walls into the figuration of the mares at Lascaux, Cixous's prose attempts to be as attentive to the surface as to the "interior," combining them into a sureness of touch that can be—as the cave paintings of Lascaux seem to be—contemporary with an unmediated knowledge of being. But for her, as well as for us, this new conflation of myth and reality is a little bit shocking. It provokes an uneasy laughter. What else can one do when the heroine whinnies?

Yet laughter, communifying and healing, like voice, is a bodily effect. And it is in terms of the body and its rhythms that translation must work. It must be Barthes's "écriture à haute voix"—"writing aloud"—"where the aim is not the clarity of messages . . . what it searches for (in a perspective of bliss) are the pulsional incidents, the language lined with flesh, . . . where we can hear the grain of the throat, the patina of consonants, the voluptuousness of vowels, a whole carnal stereophony; the articulation of the body, of the tongue, not that of meaning, of language."[7]

A tall order! One must both pay attention and let things slip through—My particular hope here has been to enter an Imaginary space where voice counts above all, to pay attention to love and let through an extravagance of violence, healing, compassion, and laughter.

1. Verena Andermatt Conley, *Hélène Cixous: Writing the Feminine* (Lincoln: University of Nebraska Press, 1984), p.139.

2. Jacques Derrida, "The Retrait of Metaphors," *Enclitic* 2 (Fall 1978): 5–33; quoted in *Difference in Translation*, ed. Joseph Graham (Ithaca: Cornell University Press, 1985), p.39.

3. Philip Lewis, "The Measure of Translation Effects," in *Difference in Translation*, p.41.

4. Conley, *Hélène Cixous,* p.146.

5. Michel Benamou, "The Concept of Marginality in Ethnopoetics," in *Minority Language and Literature: Retrospective and Perspective*, ed. Dexter Fisher (New York: Modern Language Association, 1977), p.152.

6. Lewis, "Measure of Translation Effects," p.43.

7. Roland Barthes, *The Pleasure of the Text*, trans. Richard Miller (New York: Hill and Wang), pp.66–67.

THE BOOK OF PROMETHEA

I am a little afraid for this book. Because it is a book of love. It is a burning bush. Best to plunge in. Once in the fire one is bathed in sweetness. Honestly: here I am, in it.

Very well then. I am going to try to do the introduction. Since no one wants to do it for me. Neither of the two who really made this book can bring herself to do it.

For a week H has struggled in vain. In all sincerity. As for Promethea, she is really the one who made the whole text already, the text from which I emerged just half an hour ago (my hair still clinging from the Atlantic and crystal flecks all over my body. Anyone who wants to know how this almost finished work tastes would only have to lick my shoulder).

I was saying: Promethea has already put in much that is hers and more, she drew unstintingly on her organs, her desires, her memory; the text can be said to be made, physically, morally, nervously, and above all virtuously, mostly of her.

This is not a preface. It is just half a chance to tell the truth about the origin of the text that I am in the process of leaving this very instant—refreshed, tossed about, inundated.

Maybe this is a thank-you. But technically speaking, it is genuine torture: I feel so close and yet know I am so different from H and from Promethea, I shake with a surgeon's terror. If I am not to damage the body's wonderful internal organization, the move must be as delicate as the Creator's. And I am not at all the Creator type. I am merely an author. A minor character. But I am, at least, a woman. My aim is to slip as close as possible to the two real makers' being until I can marry the contour of these women's souls with mine, without, however, causing any confusion. But in the extreme closeness sometimes necessary, it is always possible that two I's will verge on each other. I shall do whatever I can to give any sentence not from me, that might be taken for mine, back to its rightful owner.

I could have left the first page to H, who was herself the author of numerous book beginnings, but this time it might have been asking too much of her; her efforts so far have produced nothing written other than convulsions, trancelike humming, and a hypnotizing/hypnotized state; for a week she has been tormented, she burns to write something, gentle warmth emanates from her whole body, but still nothing comes of it. Besides, at the same time she is also busy burning old books, manuals, professional papers, theoretical volumes—because they keep her from doing the one thing that now seems urgent and right to her: shouting her loud hymn of ecstatic pleasure, breaching the hide of the old tongue's hard blare.

—She no longer knows where to begin: singing, burning, abolishing, liquidating, flowing, gushing; so she does it almost all at once in moist, glowing disarray. What is she thinking this very instant?

(H)—What am I going to do with my theories, all so pretty, so agile, and so theoretical, and now so obviously surrounded by reality in person in the specific person of Promethea, which they did not expect at all. Not expecting her made them secure and confirmed their very being, peacefully pastured on symbolic fields, grazing in the back of my mind where they sweetly, harmoniously whinny their satisfaction in perfect tune, combing each other's long manes unsuspecting, oh, never suspecting the surprise about to swoop down on their existence! Surprised now? Yes, not at all taken aback, but enchanted, ready to be refuted and be converted, making no distinction between abstract and concrete, without respecting the famous invisible and shimmering line between different sorts of things, the unobtainable, improbable, hence undeniable and absolutely indelible divinity.

All my more and more perfect, beautiful theories, my shuttles and my rockets, my machines rivaling in precision, wit, and temerity the toughest research brains, all the champion theories I have so carefully shaped, with such satisfaction, all of them. From the first, the one about bisexuality, which I always had some qualms about, up to the newest and supplest, the one that carried me dancing to a tune by Rossini in a single, unbroken gallop from Argel by way of Santiago to Jerusalem.

And all my theories skillfully and gracefully took up positions in my own starry night. There was an order. They obeyed my wishes so well that even though they came from me, they surprised and taught me, and even though they were no more than hypothesis and illusion, they always took me to a safe harbor as easily as any real boat. In the end, going from illusion to illusion, one also comes to understand the world. Yes. But for some time now, my theories no longer have seemed so proud and aggressive and stubborn and sometimes even solemn (like when they were full of advice about solving riddles of love). They are joyful; they make fun of each other, almost intoxicated in their freedom. They play with their own concepts, they toss them back and forth like balls.

What, in fact, is still theoretical about them (not counting the vocabulary they now use to make up nursery rhymes)? And what is a theory that is light as a butterfly, carried away by the least fragrance (and does not even theorize its lightness, but flutters around with no regrets)?

—That is what flusters H, and bothers her: She is in the process of writing off a certain way of living with dictionaries, well-ordered intellectual drawers, high-heeled shoes, jewelry, badges, degrees, funds of knowledge, etc. Officially she is dying of fear. But deep inside she stamps the ground impatiently. She is in such a hurry to dump all this baggage. But there are so many things to forget that we cannot wait for all the time it takes—at least not in this book.

—(Like you, I too have noticed the constant cropping up of horse allusions. It is a sign of the times. They are hard to curb. Because in Promethea's forests there are such beautiful, gentle mares that one does not have the heart to chase them away. And H has even come to imagine that there are some (mares) among Promethea's ancestors. One more reason not to start by turning the reins of this text over to her).

—All that because Promethea is a woman? All this uproar, this trembling, this resistance?

—Yes. No. Y-Yes . . . Naynayno. Whynoyes.

Yes, Promethea is a woman.

Yes, but "because is a woman," that is not important.

But no it is precisely its not being important that is so important.

—But who is it that claims that? Who speaks for whom?

—What I would rather say: this is not what would keep H from writing as herself.

The truth is that I am trying to find the easiest way into a book that is—I don't know how to say it—is—first, it already-is. One not written as a book because a book always anticipates somewhat its reading. This one, this book, already completely together, under this very leaf (imagine a forest under a leaf!) is entirely interior. It is so naked. Perhaps I am now clothing it a bit. That, however, is not what worries me. Perhaps I just want to protect it against hasty, precipitate incursions: since it doesn't have a wall or a coat one might end up inside by chance, or fall right in without going to the trouble of reading it.

But I may also be afraid.

I am afraid.

I have already read it. And, not to lie to you, I liked it. But I am afraid. I am not afraid of you, Fidelia, Sania, Ania. I am afraid of *you*.

(I put all this in my separate notebook. My doubtbook.)

This is a naked book, as exposed as Promethea. In its writing it never thought of being read later. I am afraid for it. Yet Promethea never even thinks of being afraid.

It is so naked.

It is innocent. It never asks itself the questions people ask themselves—and it is right—this is no place to ask them.

Innocent as Promethea. (Since it comes from her.)

First, never has Promethea thought of saying: "I am a woman." (Though she is . . .) No, the truth is: Promethea

IS. Is Promethea. (Inside IS—so wonderful.) (The book that follows is inside her. It is maybe even her womb itself.)

But I am just a woman who thinks her duty is not to forget. And this duty, which I believe I must fulfill, is: "as a woman" living now I must repeat again and again "I am a woman," because we exist in an epoch still so ancient and ignorant and slow that there is still always the danger of gynocide.

That is what I believe. That is what I believe, I believe personally. I believe and it is my duty to believe, and I owe it to all the veiled women in the world to believe that I must still stubbornly utter the magical, unveiling credential words "I am a woman." When? As often as necessary and possible. And especially when I start to build a new house or start a new book, with my ritual anxious groping. Or especially at the groping, clumsy beginnings of a fragile, temporary city, pulled alive but shivering all over with shyness, out of my imaginary earth. Especially at the beginnings of this doubtful region, this thing, this crazy creature, this mirage that is stronger than I, this uncontrollable child, who obeys and disobeys me, comes from me and leaves me, and who scarcely having left, gets away, rises, mountain, gallops, and immediately I have to start climbing, straddling, I have to try to catch her. But no wishful thinking: she is barely up and already far away, I the archer, she the arrow.

So then, how can I make my arrow not completely free of the past; so that it keeps a trace of my desire, of its provenance? The only thing that comes to mind is to carve a little motto on its shaft, like: "I come from a woman."

I am dropping the arrow now. It is only a metaphor. I wish I could lay all weapons down.

—Because, really I am a little tired of this besieged existence. I feel like a tiny state surrounded by twenty opposing states. From birth it has screamed with all its ego shouting itself hoarse: "I exist, I am, don't come near, I have teeth, I have claws." Shouts itself hoarse and has a sore throat and sore shoulders and sore eyes and would like to stop dressing in steel, and I would like to sleep naked on warm sand beside her very own sea. I would like to doze now on Promethea's shore, without weapons, without worry, without memory, without apprehension. I would like so much to be a woman without giving it a thought. I would like so much to be the freest of free women: so free that I would even be liberated from the painful sensation of being-liberated. I would like to be so freely free that I would never even think to say to myself: "How free I am!" because it is just something I would be. Purely, absolutely, I would be free, I would be, and that's all, I would be H, I would be stretched out alongside Promethea, and I would sleep; it would be perfectly beautiful, and I would wake up, on Promethea's shore, and I wouldn't turn around with a shudder. No one would be behind me, no one above us, I wouldn't jump up with a start, I wouldn't reach my hand out to grab a piece of paper, a shield, a rifle, a pen. There would be the sea, there would be peace and the earth, there would be nobody or lots of people. I would sing or not sing, all depending on the rhythm of my blood. I would breathe deeply the grassy scent of Promethea spread out in the sun; that would last a very, very long time, because above the sea, above the earth, above us, there would also be plenty of time.

But I am no freest of the free. I am just free enough to dream of being so. And enough to be able to guess the extreme rarity, the lightness of air where Promethea's ideas find their inspiration.

Because Promethea goes to sleep and wakes up unguarded.

She is so naturally unguarded, yes, so innocent of weapons that sometimes I am even a little embarrassed before her, I feel almost shameless confronting her nakedness, I who am girded in suspicions, am feathered in forebodings, arguments, word constructions, loaded down with expectations, with experience, with a memory that is heavy and impure.

How can this difference be shown?

It is as if I were dreaming about Freedom. It is as if I were giving a course on Freedom in my dream. And I do not know how to talk about it, I do not even know the first word of what I ought to know; the audience is there, I am looking for the Book, I do not even know what language I am supposed to speak. I am beside myself, in front of everyone. Outside I am guilty and inside I am guilty, and while I leaf, hopeless and humiliated, through an illegible, annotated manual, suddenly, I see the great magical mare move through the depths of my dream; from behind my desk, my bars and my tormenters. I see silver lightning striking over there, far away, and that is what it is—Freedom herself, You, Promethea, you go by and I stay in the depths of my dream lit up and silent as a rock. But this rosy silver light caresses my stone, penetrates my pain, deep into my guts.

Oh, soften and impregnate me, melt me!

I, the undersigned "author," come from the following book on behalf of H, who is presently incapable of making the burning words come out of her breast.

"Author" is a pseudonym that should fool no one.

(Note to Promethea on the book's way of doing things)

Here, I think, I ought to try raising the question of my division between I and H.

I ask Promethea's permission to be slightly two, or slightly more, slightly unsettled, as long as I have neither succeeded in living and writing precisely where I live and, hence, succeeded in being myself, the same woman who lives and writes nor openly decided in favor of one of my two possibilities.

At the moment I am inclined to favor union. But currently, in these pages brought on by my remorse or my mistrust, I still live first and write later, off to the side a bit, often perched at the level of the first tree branches, keeping an eye on all three horizons, ready to fly off at the first sign of danger, leaving H, my first person, to cope with questioning by reporters and police. I almost argued with Promethea over this. She made no bones about reproaching me for my little maneuver. That, at least, is how I took her surprise at seeing I had reserved two places for myself in the text (so I would be able to slip continually from one to the other), and I cried. Yes, after brief hesitation, I decided the incident worthy of tears. So it was almost serious.

It is still beyond my forces, I still don't have quite enough nerve. I am—or was until now—an author who has always worked hard to transform reality into fiction; out of equal respect for reality and for fiction, I felt obliged to be wary of any attempt at representation, and that made me always want to keep writing at some distance from life itself (at least that is what I thought I wanted to do—but I cannot judge the result).

I tried to write decently . . . Etc.

—I'll stop: who I was does not interest me. Who I am in the process of being is strange and breathtaking to me. To tell the truth I am scared to death. It is delicious. I cannot even say that I am writing or have written this book that is waiting for us, breathlessly new (panting) behind the page—even if I put the words on the page, this book took off by itself, and it has been a marvelous ride for me—I never thought I would end up on the back of a mare.

I mention riding because that was how the book provided me with the most amazing thrills. And that was when I understood I was letting myself be carried along by a vital force far greater than my own. All I did was to follow the fabulous route on a map of the world. And so this book comprises the expedition's itinerary as well, which is the only part of it directly produced by me. But the current of an immense river has also swept me away, moved me, lulled and rolled me, set me down, overturned and fished me back out. And while there I was never afraid. And sometimes my womb, too, was the carrier, and I took things across.

All that to tell you, Promethea, that I have new problems with this book: because up to now I was the one who wrote my books for the most part, at least as far as form was concerned. I made decisions rather early. I did not impose a ready-made mold. But I let motifs, melodies, dimensions, colors, suggest themselves to me, like a good architect who considers all the geographical and historical features and the innermost requirements of the divinity that is to reveal itself, in the temple. And it will only be able to manifest itself and deliver its oracle if the place permits. So I began by listening to the heartbeat of the divinity.

But this time, perhaps, divinity does not need my services. I feel uncomfortable, almost redundant, slightly skittish, very cheery, tempted by irresponsibility, the idea of being marginally the author of a book that is ahead of me, delights and frightens me. Because I really do have a sense of responsibility. I certainly do not want to wrongly benefit from a work that I am only part of. But neither do I want to be spared the dangers of bringing out something so risky.

I am having trouble with this book. But this book has none with itself, and none with Promethea.

Why am I afraid? Because this is a Children's book. Capital C Children. Big Children. Of every age, type, or race.

Because it is a book of love. Sometimes I call it the Book of Rages. It is a raging book. One must leap in. Once in the fire one is bathed in sweetness.

Because it is a book about now . . . to read for no reason. Without asking: "then what? what happens at the end?" Because there is no ending.

Because it is a fearless book. Besides, that is what makes it impossible for H to have written it alone. Nor could I have.

Besides it is Promethea's book. It is the book Promethea lit like a fire in H's soul.

Promethea does not understand why I let H in here, when the book was already so lush in bloom around us. I do not know how to explain. I had no choice. There are moments when I am H. I do not really want to be. I am just trying not to stop the flow of the text, even if I have almost passed out with passion.

But the one passing out the most is H.

I said this book is entirely internal. When the author that I am feels the need to build a circumferential or a scaffolding or to weave a silken tent, it is perhaps not to her credit.

Promethea is my heroine.

But the question of writing is my adversary.

Promethea is the heroine of my life, of my imagination, of my book.

I am her champion. I fight for her, to make her right—her reality, her presence, her grandeur—prevail.

I am armed with love and care. Which is not enough.

Sometimes I need to add writing as well. Promethea is so tall. Writing helps me. I climb on her.

But writing then immediately demands to be paid, and I am not exactly sure what this payment should be.

Strange things happen: I write to come close to Promethea; I seek her better, more slowly, more closely, more deeply. But then I begin to lose the surface, the simplicity and light.

That is serious.

It can go far. It can go too far.

Other strange things happen: each page I write could be the first page of the book. Each page is completely entitled to be the first page. How is this possible?

Because this is a day-by-day book, each day, the one happening now, is the most important day. For each day I need all time.

Because we are in eternity.

We. Promethea, me, the author, H, you and you, whoever wants, whoever loves us, whoever loves.

This whole book is composed of first pages.

For the author that is serious.

Sometimes, also, it is troublesome and painful. It gives me a headache: I would like Promethea to pick a page to be first, the way one picks up a shell on the beach.

The miracle: I have noticed that I can say almost nothing about Promethea in her absence. Because, in her absence, she is really absent. And what I live then is: absence-of-Promethea. I see her dimmed by absence. Nothing can make her radiant again. I am loath to make her up by applying words.

To talk about her I need her, and not her image, close by. I need to open the window and call her with my voice. I am afraid, when she is not there, that writing will carry me away, far from her, far from myself, far from writing, far from truth.

This miracle is also a nuisance. After all, I can't just write from life, can I?

Is that not what I always do? Write on what is alive? But up to now I thought of myself as writing on paper. Sometimes the paper was thick enough, in fact, for me not to feel the blood flowing under the skin, under the paper.

I open my notebook, I open the window, I call, and my heroine is there, really. I am overwhelmed.

I warn her: "I am writing on you, Promethea, run away, escape. I am afraid to write you, I am going to hurt you!"

But rather than run away, she comes at a gallop. Through the window she comes, breathing hard, and alive as can be, she flings herself into the book, and there are bursts of laughter and splashes of water everywhere, on my notebook, on the table, on my hands, on our bodies.

Which is why I said: it is a book completely in the present. It began to be written the moment the present began—long before I understood that a book was being made. I have been out of my depth ever since. Am I maybe trying now to bring it back to familiar shores? Is that why Promethea disapproves of me? She thinks it is beautiful the way it is. But I am afraid of this beauty. I am afraid to be right. I am also afraid that she is right. I am so torn that I wake up in the morning my shoulders racked.

The question driving me mad is: how can one manage to be simultaneously inside and outside?

I want to avoid tricks. I am certainly aware that I frighten Promethea when I let myself go on talking in two voices (actually only one of the two speaks audibly, the other is unheard-of). I am trying to put myself in Promethea's place. How would I feel if I thought she was two living persons? I don't know. With my extendable soul, with my person-plus-shadow, I have trouble putting myself in the place of someone who is of the magnitude of one, even if her size, the scale of her soul, her height, is that of a people in its combined forces. Promethea is a people. I am the one who is only two, one of them a shadow.

So, is H my shadow? I don't know that either. I take her to be my shadow, but certain people feel I am her shadow. So does that make me the shadow of my shadow? I can see how that might be disagreeable. When you love a person, you don't love her shadow.

But I could say H is my night person. She is more willing to be submerged than I. She lets herself become a little impersonal, whereas I am afraid of getting lost. I prefer being on the mare's back rather than in the cave she came from, where the earliest musics echo. But H is all set to venture into my Paleolithic, all the way into the Chamber of Mares. When it is too dark down the Shaft where H is dreaming, like now, and if, nonetheless, one wants to hear the music, one must take along the rosy stoneware lamp where little twigs of juniper burn, lighting up the Cave of the Soul to a depth of fifteen thousand years.

Thoughts build up like tears in H's breast—she is not awake, but she is not sleeping: she floats, hardly moving, not far from the edges of this text where she lies soaking—her thoughts have the same mellow salty taste as the glowing liquid that fills the nearly spherical membrane of this "story." . . .

I lay my face on H's breast. I hear tears trickling down the walls of the Chamber. It smells good: she must be dreaming of the mare's flanks. Each time the mare goes past in a dream, you can tell because of this odor that fills the night. Today just like fifteen thousand years ago. Today fifteen thousand years ago.

I hear:

H: "Now here I am . . ."

(Listen, Promethea, this is the first line of one of the first pages of the book inside. Therefore, H must be somewhere in the Hall. The inner book is laid out astonishingly like the site of Lascaux. Promethea is the one who discovered that. The same division into three principle chambers or chapters and galleries corresponding to the eight epochs. But in all of them one finds frescoes in the Magdalenian style characterized by its free drawing, the action-filled bodies, and the aura of eternity marking all the scenes caught in their stunning, momentary immediacy. Wait:

I still have something to say about why H needs to be in this text. H comes slightly before me; she dates from my personal antiquity, she is thus both older and younger than I. From the point of view of my subjective archaeology, she is situated in the preconscious, in a rather childish state of receptivity: she is preceded by the world. Yes. The world comes first, she is plunged into it, it cradles her, lashes her, laps at her, and she perceives, perceives. A female embryo that is at the center of life, she hears all, feels all, yet has never yet seen anything. But a female embryo, already thinking and speaking: if only she could be born at will!)

I listen some more:

H: "So exceedingly hard to hoist oneself out of the silky womb of the present and tie a tiny strand of golden thread at the mouth of this cave, so others can see which way to venture,

. . . It makes me cry, I want to talk about something I am not sure I can talk about, I want to talk about the inside from inside, I do not want to leave it

I am so happy in the silky damp dark of the labyrinth and there is no thread

So exceedingly hard to invent the tiniest slip of golden thread to hoist outside as a sign: here, this way to where we can make up our minds to slip into the narrative.

(The narrative? What narrative? If only it were a narrative! But it is precisely not a narrative, it is time, burning time, beating from hour to hour, it is time beating in life's breast).

I am painfully like a womanfish who has decided that now it is time to look the sea in its face.

All flexed and anguished, she wrings her fins and spreads them wide—to no avail, she only surfaces between two waves and still has no wings.

It makes me drool (H moans), the minute I open my mouth I dribble metaphors, "forest," "narrative," "womanfish," it is all pretend, taking advantage of my disarray, because I have no idea how to get out while staying in, I don't know how, I don't want to enough, I am so happy in the intoxicating and cosmic womb of the present! And yet I want to present this present—to whom?—to those I love, because, to my mind, it is a realm worth giving, it is an inner India, a natural palace, a country of magnificent contours—in short, all I want to say, very quickly, before the metaphors swoop straight down on my heart to steal its blood, is that I have found the entrance to a life so rich in personal events, one so stirred up, so potent and nascent, a life that never stops bursting into lives, into shouts of life, into tears of life, into laughs of life, into songs of life, into terrors of life,

the entrance, naturally, is close by, just like in stories and like in reality, it is extremely close, it is right here, here in the garden, even closer, in the house, in the breast, even closer?—even closer . . .

(moans H, body arched, scales glittering with sweat, fins

spread wide, gills throbbing, trying, at the risk of bursting, to make the transition from the realm of water to the realm of words)

. . . I did not even know this existed . . . this world, I did not know. I thought it existed only in one's head, and in dreams . . . . And now: here I am.

H went to lie down, to rest or maybe after this exhausting foray to the outside, to immerse herself again deep in her vital innermost recesses and immediately felt herself slip into the soft, sensory interior of the present which welcomed her in again, rocked her, and made peace with her. And it was true that she was drooling over it. A trickle of blood oozed from her mouth. And she pulled away from the outside like someone leaving only a sloughed-off outer skin to mark her place on earth. But inside she went back to joy; inside; there where life, carefree, without restraint, shouted her great cries of victory; inside she regained her strength and her calm, because she could peacefully inhale the vital violence of life there without false modesty; and she could yell freely, yell her admiration and her terror . . .

For the time being I cannot do without H. I do not yet have the mental courage to be only *I*. I dread nothing as much as autobiography. Autobiography does not exist. Yet so many people believe it exists. So here I solemnly state: autobiography is only a literary genre. It is nothing living. It is a jealous, deceitful sort of thing—I detest it. When I say "I," this I is never the subject of autobiography, my I is free. Is the subject of my madness, my alarms, my vertigo.

I is the heroine of my fits of rage, my doubts, my passions. I lets itself go. I let myself go. I surrenders, gets lost, does not comprehend itself. Says nothing about me. I does not lie. I do not lie to anyone. I does not lie to anyone, I promise: that is why I has almost nothing to say about me—which raises some doubt as to the balance or harmony of the book.

In fact, there is no limit to what I can say about Promethea—other than the reader's weariness.

But about me? No. Who could speak about "me," if not myself, and since I am "the author"?

That is a burning question. Personally, I still don't have the answer.

But Promethea has one. She asks me to write that she loves me.

(I am a bit ashamed because I feel so much resistance, I disobey her, she has already asked me several times if I really did what she asked me to do. I sort of lied. I said, "I'm getting ready to. I'm going to." But it's as if she wanted me to caress myself, it makes my wrists cramp up. Yet it's not the same thing. All the same, this demands a humility I do not possess. The more she trusted, the more impossible it was to obey. Until, yesterday, when she took my papers. She read them and, luckily, I saw how sad it made her. Otherwise, shamefully, fearfully, secretly, I would have kept on being evasive. And she murmured sadly, "You never wrote that I love you?" And her eyes were like tears. And I understood how stingy and cheap and arrogant and ungracious I had been. Because it is easy to love and sing one's love. That is something I am extremely good at doing. Indeed, that is my art. But to be loved, that is true greatness. Being loved, letting oneself be loved, entering the magic and dreadful circle of generosity, receiving gifts, finding the right thank-you's, that is love's real work.

Yesterday I made Promethea the sincere promise that I would sincerely do my best to write what she wants.

It is a promise.

Which is an even newer, even greater difficulty than all the others.

Perhaps building a circumferential around a garden spoils it. Perhaps it is as bad a calculation as the invasion of Lebanon. Perhaps it is destruction under the pretext of protection. Perhaps it is precluding under the pretext of preserving. Two conceptions of the work are in confrontation: out of skepticism and distrust regarding the human race, I am for the protection of nature. Promethea trusts everything: nature, the human race, me, herself. This is a controversial problem.

But writing a book with another book growing inside is what makes a revolutionary issue of the practice of . . . I have no idea what word to use.

Obviously I am not concerned with the author's rights.

It is how serious translation is that torments me. Translating oneself is already serious—I mean putting life into words—sometimes it is almost putting it to death; sometimes dragging it out, sometimes embalming it, sometimes making it vomit or lie, sometimes bringing it to climax, but one never knows before beginning whether one's luck will be good or bad, whether this is birth or suicide. But translating someone else—that requires extraordinary arrogance or extraordinary humility. Extraordinary arrogance is something I don't have. And extraordinary humility—I don't know who has that. Except perhaps Promethea. In this book (expanding and growing richer as I sit here stewing), which is Promethea's book, a young, vigorous book is growing, one I don't know how to write.

————Because I am not Promethea, and I cannot bring myself to act as if I were, I am not a real liar, I cannot ascribe my words to her without feeling that this poisons and invents her.

So what am I to do? I can take down Promethea's words under dictation. That is a possibility. But not good enough. Because Promethea has the idea that I know better than she what she wants to say, when she speaks to me silently with her eyes, her mouth, the corners of her lips, her hands, and everything she confides in me in her other tongues. But I have my doubts, about myself and about words as well: I am not sure my written language can faithfully translate all the many living, original, cosmic, personal languages.

All I can promise is to take down faithfully the words Promethea says out loud in French. As for all the rest, I make no guarantees.

Today, first I am going to do what Promethea wants. (But I won't tell her until the end of the day. Even with her I am modest. Now I feel as superstitious as when faced with a freezing ocean: "Dive in!" I tell myself, "or else something awful will happen to the one you hold dear!" And right up to the last thousandth of a second my own flesh struggles and pleads and claims that it is dearer to itself than the other's life is, and then complains of blackmail and accuses me of superstition, but my soul eventually makes it understand: this isn't superstitious, it is a test. Would you give your skin to your dear? (All this is, of course, concealed too in the indefinite pronoun "one.") I dive in. But sometimes I put the dive off to another lifetime.

That's it, here I go.

I dove in. And I not only wrote the words from Promethea that come next, but I also said them to my mother, in spite of my misgivings.

Promethea's words:

"Tell your mother that I love you enough to die for you."

It's done.

My mother said, "Those are words."

And then she said something else that I swear I've forgotten. It went something like this: "Some people have enthusiastic dispositions, which makes for obligations." She meant something like "Noblesse oblige." It is true. I am ready and willing too, Promethea. I am so ready that I could tell my mother on your behalf, in your honor, words I dare not say to my mother, that I dare not write, words I think you are crazy to think, that I think you are even crazier to say. I am ready to say that with your life you think things of fire, even if I know that nowadays these are called "words."

You oblige me, Promethea. I am under obligation to you.

This book is my obliging you. This is a book I never would have dared write, if I did not feel protected and obligated by your madness. I am writing it just behind the burning bush, by the light of your blaze. You crackle softly and I write it down.

You are obligated to yourself, I know that. There are words with obligations. There are sentences that carry the person who spoke them galloping away, in a foaming race to the edge of the earth. There, if one has lied, the sentences turn back into wind, the words are reduced to ashes, and one falls into the void, without being able to utter a cry.

Those sentences are untranslatable. Perhaps they are not true sentences. They are truth's omnipotent mares. Those who lie and try to take them for their own will break their necks.

But my mother's sentences are hasty translations, translatable, somewhat slapdash.

Luckily, Promethea is untranslatable. That is my one consolation; she races on in an out-of-breath language that is, for me, unbearable. Every time she tosses something out it is so impassioned and so sudden, it is so naked, that each time I shudder as if she had handed me a heart taken fresh from someone's breast; and I say to myself almost reproachfully: "how can one say that?" "I would never say that myself!" A reproach to whom? I don't know, I don't know.

All the things I don't know anymore because of Promethea!

So many things I knew and no longer know anymore. . . .

At least there will be no room for confusion: Promethea's speech is very simple and high and very pointed like a mountain. She uses few words because there are few at that altitude but they are sparkling and transparent like glaciers at the very top. Her vocabulary comes always from the guts, hers or the earth's. It comes out smoking and violent, with roots still permeated with blood, with earth, with salt, with oil.

But she also uses gentler forms, ancient recitations that

ripple out along the road, in airy notes, in rainbowed bubbles of sound, leaving silver traces in the air. Generally, her languages are ancient and fresh and lightly limned as the paintings at Lascaux. They are all clairvoyant. She speaks in evocations and eruptions more than in metaphors. Whereas I, I drill, I dig, I sink in, I plow even the sea, I want to turn it over.

No, we do not speak at all the same languages. Things she lets bubble up in a shower of sparks, I would like to collect and bind. She burns and I want to write out the fire! Luckily, I'll never succeed.

I will set myself to it. This is what I want, I confess, Promethea has awakened in me dreams extinguished for thousands of years; sometimes one catches on fire even through so many icy layers. Promethea has rekindled dreams of fire in me, dreams of abysses, they are terribly dangerous dreams: as long as they are dreams alone, as long as one dreams alone, one can fool around with dreaming, because afterward one forgets. But now, ever since I learned how Promethea brings the fire of all dreams up into reality, how she climbs back up through the shaft of the Red Cows, bearing the first fire, how she crosses the Chamber of the Mares, how she goes through every epoch of existence reawakening along the walls memories of times so fragile and so inflammable, and comes out in 1982 still carrying in her hands the primitive spark, I feel myself wavering between exultation and terror. Formerly, I too sucked satiny coals. Once I burned my tongue. (That only happens if someone makes you lose faith.) Ever since I have no longer dared suck real fire; for a long time I lived on electricity. But I have never forgotten the fiery taste of eternity. I just was sure that I could live with my tongue extinguished until the end of my days. I was not even tempted. I was calm. I had firm definitions. I called happiness the absence of unhappiness. I wrote in ink and I dedicated my dreams to the Moons.

And now, I am tempted, I revel in temptation, I intend to crawl furtively to the dish of coals but I am no longer three years old, I want to eat, but I also want to sing. I don't know, can one do both at the same time?

Yes, Promethea is her true name.

Promethea said to me: I would like to spend three years with the tribe, I would like to learn their arts, their carpentry, the way they build frames with trees twelve feet off the ground and the secret of the twelve colors they use and of their delicate, gigantic frescoes; I would like to spend three years speaking their language and collecting their recipes.

I pictured it. My guts knotted and I said: I can't. I need paper, my books, pens. To say nothing of light. And also the telephone.

We had a long, sad, three-year autumn.

It even bothers me right now, while I am writing these lines to defend—in some ways—my defensive attitude and to justify my devious means—at that moment necessary for me, strategic, somewhat painful—but, I believe, or fear, also indispensable—so it bothers me, I am saying, to set up this glacis which is small but probably ugly, so close to Promethea, because I know what she is going to think of it: she is not going to like it. For her ramparts are a nuisance. When I submitted the plan of my initial fortifications to her a week ago (it was the pages of introduction I had just constructed—with which I was not unhappy: for me, without these props, the crumbly, soft earth of the present would have threatened to collapse with the first slightly heavy reader who tried it) she reacted so suddenly that I lost my balance.

I had barely put down the last word and she said: "I don't like that at all! That's literature. I don't recognize any of it anymore." And she snorted furiously, and neighed so angrily that even today I get chills.

I said: "I know I'm right. And you're wrong."

I said that because it was my right and my duty to think: I

know and I'm right. My right and my duty as a hardworking woman. But her right and her duty were to tell me I was wrong. But pleasing cannot be done by force. And when one is not pleasing one is wrong. I said. "I'm wrong. But. I'm right." I said that for myself. So as not to abandon myself. But I did not know what I knew.

And that was the first time we were alone. Each of us began to feel a rush of vague, irritated thoughts, as capricious as ghosts, spreading in nightmarish confusion, thoughts arising from the barbaric beginnings of their humanity. Each of us thought she felt a forgotten ancestor waking up at the bottom of her twenty-thousand-year-old cave. We each had goose bumps. Did one of us, perhaps, repress a growl? We suddenly saw each other twenty thousand years ago, I am sure, and we ran away from each other, terror-stricken by love. Because otherwise I would have shown you my teeth? In any case we heard thought sigh: "I would like to exist twenty thousand years from now!"

Each of us wanted to die.

Then we were each very tired.

Then we each thought about the mystery of love.

And we didn't understand at all.

We didn't argue. But for once we had taken two different paths to get through the forest. I was afraid. This fear made it dark. I was afraid of bumping into Promethea in the dark.

For the first time I left a little before she did, before the sun, in darkness (because I'm not saying I saw clearly, but for me darkness has always been the promise of another light). I went away to forget. Or I went away to think. I went away to go away.

Walking through my own darkness, I thought and thought, I took a whole walk of thought, in silence (in *my* silence, because I am not saying I did not hear Promethea galloping in the nearby trees and the rustling of leaves that violently caressed her flanks).

I thought as I distanced myself from Promethea,

because I thought things that I could not think right next to her unless it was against her,

I thought as I distanced myself from my own heart, because I thought things that I cannot think about except through distant, impersonal allusions, otherwise they would turn back against me to embed themselves like poisoned needles in my breast,

I left to think the worst, I left looking for the worst in the forest, thinking: I will fight, whether I get lost, whether I win, whether I'm right or wrong, I want to go and think what I fear.

Then I thought first:

"Promethea frightens me." And I was afraid. She frightens me because she can knock me down with a word. Because she does not know that writing is walking on a dizzying silence setting one word after the other on emptiness. Writing is miraculous and terrifying like the flight of a bird who has no wings but flings itself out and only gets wings by flying. She doesn't know how I tremble with terror and certainty. Because to write is to work with a certainty that is demoniacal, solely, shakily, demoniacal, and yet to work with absolute confidence.

I am just as sure as I am uncertain. And I can't tell you this, Promethea.

I feel like a sleepwalker who *knows* that she is walking on the edge of the abyss while sound asleep.

But if she is the only one who knows, she will sleepwalk without falling. If she is the only one who knows, she can also not know it. I know I'm asleep, Promethea, don't wake me up too fast.

I'm sad and I feel a little sick at my stomach because I am afraid right now that Promethea doesn't want to follow my footsteps sleepwalking, and consequently can't understand me. On the one hand, as far as my writing (and not myself) is concerned, it is all right with me, it has to be all right with me.

But on the other hand, as far as I, my living I, is concerned, if she did not understand me I would be destroyed.

On the one hand I have nothing to lose, I hope for nothing, I want no other god than the idea I have of not-lying. Only to this god am I responsible.

On the other, I have everything to lose, life, joy, beauty. It is terrible, it is exhilarating, and it is good, that's how it is.

I don't want to lie, Promethea, I don't want to make a mistake. I want to live. I am so happy, Promethea, that you cause me so much anxiety, that you give me so much to lose! So much to want not to lose!

Such a battle is going on inside me! And I don't know whose side to pray for. I still don't know. There is going to be a victory, that I know, I am the one who is going to lose, but I am the one who is going to win.

Please, Promethea, wait for me, let me have time to take an interior route, which is my inevitable path, I won't take long to come out, and then I will give you news from the interior.

I kept going through the forest.

I thought, writing is a solitary act, but what does "solitary" mean?

No, I thought more specifically: writing is a translation. But isn't everything in life translation? But certain translations are eloquent with words. Others with visions. I see you translating, Promethea, I see you translating us at the precise moment in which we, we go by.

Is the difference that I translate slightly after the event? But I translate with love, in minute detail; my madness lies, perhaps, in wanting to translate almost everything. So is it perhaps a heavy, or slow translation that I produce?

But next week, as soon as I finish building up my edges, I swear I will translate differently, with great, brilliant, rapid strokes. I thought: every act is "solitary." Cooking too is a solitary act. Just as solitary, just as unsolitary as writing. I am writing while I imagine the moment you will taste what I have fixed for you. I am cooking spicy, fragrant words for you, I am writing Hindu, I love spicy writing.

I like to cook for you. I like you to cook for me. I like to make you taste my strangeness. Your complicated, complex taste delights me, you speak seven harmonious tongues to me in one mouthful.

Sometimes, when I cook for you I speak to you in some Far Eastern tongue that brings a cosmic smile to your lips, sometimes I speak to you in Chinese and you understand, sometimes it comes from Angkor, which is good. But sometimes you don't like my dish: is it because I have spoken too strange a tongue? It is a highly seasoned language, I agree. I need that: it is a language with which I have had to mix an antidote, a European language, threatened with exile, with prison. I fear for it.

I fear for us. I dare not speak it undefended in this country. I need to speak it sheltered behind a low oriental wall.

I kept going, still in the forest, but it was slightly less dark (and I smelled the fragrance of Promethea's mane floating in the shrubbery along rustling limbs; so, we're getting closer).

Then I thought, Promethea thinks we don't need weapons. And in fact, she herself is never armed. It is fair to say that since she is always dreaming at an altitude of thousands of feet, she has no idea of the dangers of urban sleepwalking. One can get killed when one's dreams are only three stories high.

I think disarmament would be a mistake.

Doesn't Promethea dream of an Edenic disarmament of Israel, all the while grieving over the inevitability of arms?

On this subject she knows how to waver.

But I too waver, I change my mind.

I thought, I'm right.

Now I think, "Suppose she was right?"

It is right for me to think that, at least, as a hypothesis.

I ask to be granted yet a few more pages of patience . . .

(I need to exonerate myself, Promethea: I am not guilty, but I am not innocent. My offense is in feeling accusable.)

There are still three or four small chambers I want to take you through in my labyrinth, and then there will be only the great treasure room. Entirely present. Entirely pure and clear.

In the first stark, dark chamber, seventy-five feet down, I announce:

That is raw eternity shining at the end of the gallery. It is a sort of luminous book with, perhaps, not the slightest need for my circumlocutions.

I behave like the poet who had the word "god" come to his lips before an "absolutely modern" audience in Moscow in 1932; the word, not the noun, and it was scandalous; he simply meant to say: human, infinitely human. And this poet, who did not believe in God the God, wanted to cry he was so distressed, and wanted to believe in God. And he never again wanted to speak this word, which had become precious and fragile as a baby, except in the presence of the only one he loved.

The way I behave is to cast glances all around me, to see if the world's eyes could reflect the brilliance of a burst of the honey air that is Promethea's aura.

I do my behaving in 1982.

This is how I behave outwardly.

But inside everything is set free. There is no date. Inside it is Saturday. Day of nakedness. Day of presence. Every language is a good one, voices are apt, words are neither required nor repressed.

Outside I behave: with mistrust, memories, metastases.

I have three memories: the Paleolithic, the biblical, the poetic. I am a creature of three species. Each species is threatened with extinction. Watch over my coals, Promethea, keep an eye on my three satin hearts. I have three fears. I have one fear from my father, the Jew; I have a three-thousand-year-old fear from his memory and the memory of his people, and from the memory of miracled peoples, miraculable, not yet miracled, perhaps never again to be miracled, peoples yet un-miracled, people at sea, people to the sharks; I have a fear from peoples who slowly, heavily, silently have been sinking into memory at a speed of two centimeters a year since 1917, and already now, through the thin layer of earth what they are saying can just barely be heard; I have a fear from peoples whose only line is a red alert. I have this fear because I belong to the species of peoples threatened with miracles. Also with nonmiracle miracles.

I don't rest easy on this earth. There is a small external organ on my body where I hurt. I have a slightly hysterical geographical nature. I have a small uterus that contracts too often, east of my stomach. Every morning I am struck with amazement: I am still there! Everyday at noon I argue with my mother about these middle-eastern uterine contractions. Every night I dive into the fathomless depths of history, I swim five thousand years, I remember, I forget, a dark Nile rocks me, I wonder: would you be there, Promethea, among the estuary reeds, will you be there tomorrow morning five thousand years from now to take me, soaking wet, from the murky shadows, will you get there precisely that day, that moment, at that bend in the river, in that clump of reeds, coming from the other side of the world, will you be there with barefeet in thin sandals, solemnly on your long legs, the legs of another species of woman? will you just happen to come to this very spot, to this pinprick on the globe? will you lean over with your face the color of a different sun than mine? will you see me with your eyes the color of such a foreign tongue?

I interrupted myself . . . I have to note the exact time and place because it is right here that Promethea made me leave the small, dark chamber and took me on a fabulous trip, to the end of a long day of initiation, along a river with saffron waters, one so broad of body that you could not see from one bank to the other. And reeds bound the riverbanks. And it was as if Promethea had led my adult, living self to be present at my own birth, my own awakening, when I was taken from the waters.

Back to where I left off: I am in the next small chamber—you would think it was the same, just as dark and free of adornment. And it is the same sort of question, the same ordeal, the same agony. The question of birth, of nonbirth, of Noluck.

How close I came to not being alive. To not being born. A matter of one day. One train. One bit of luck. One slowing of the wheel of Fortune. I made it by a centimeter. The hour I was born a poet died in Tcherdyn in the destiny nearby. I am unable to forget. My memory is uneven. My memory adopts. A memory camp spreads out in my memory. I would like my memory to die and come back virgin. I would like to wash my memory in forgetting. But my memory does not close well, my memory's wall has cracks in it. Other people's recollections, coincidences, affinities migrate against my will. I remember the arrest of Liova on my seventh birthday, as if it were yesterday and as if I were her mother, as if my legs were swollen in foreknowledge of the twenty years of waiting, standing in agonizing lines, as if mine were the blue eyes almost black with wrath, as if an eternal blood song had risen in my throat in a strange tongue, in a common, furious, mother tongue. I am a maternal, feline, furious sort of woman. Luckily. I am a woman in black, my memory salty with tears, there are veils drying in the harsh sun on the terrace of my memory. How close! A matter of one street, one race, a century, a woman encountered, a sea crossed and I would not be walking so erect, so personal, so inside myself, in the midst of the nation among nations. How close I came to not being me, to not being who I was born. How close I came to being only the vague shadow of who I am.

That is why I still tell what is, with the astonishment of any little girl who explores. I discover my own being with loud

Galilean shouts. I am still astronomical to myself. I shout: "A star! A Woman! She spins! She lives!" Yes, I am not used to it. It drives me wild. I am all excited, spinning round and round I run, I am exhausting. But I am new. I am fearful but triumphant. I exist. I want to make sure. I want simply to be a proof, one small proof among millions, my own proof of the existence of women.

—I think Promethea does not try to prove. She is. Yet she is for me not only a proof of women, but a proof of—of the divinity of the human race. No—I meant of "the femininity" of the human race. But in the end, I no longer know what to call it when a person makes you believe in something you have no reason, either biblical, modern, archaic, Judaic, historical, or political, to believe: in the possibility of survival for a species that is able to keep its radiant savage nature all the way into the black heart of culture; or perhaps in the existence of an innocence that is more powerful than any court. Promethea is perfectly improbable. And yet *si muove*.

That is why H sometimes calls Promethea *Eppur* or *E pur*, calls her "And yet . . .," "purely is." Pure pleasure in wordplay. And also because we, H and I, know too well how far from innocence I was born. Everything I am comes with: "I know this is what I am."

What do I know about being simply I-Whoever, without H, without fear, and without proof!

But I cannot do that yet. For example, I am concealing some misgivings behind my heart as far as Promethea's book is concerned.

My misgiving is, I am afraid that a malevolent reading will cast an evil eye on us. I don't want to go into all that now. As for H, she is only killing herself with going outside and waving just to say "over here, come, here I am"—because she is submitting to scruples that are not even hers, but rather those of her close, friendly, advice-giving friends: because when she discovered the entrance of the Present Absolute, she felt such a blaze of joy that every shadow of wisdom, prudence, and precaution vanished before its brilliant glow; and when she rushed to bring her best friendly friends to the entrance, a fearless soul, as if the whole world were also the divine Uterus, which is simply not the case—to share the passage with them and invite them this way, this way; to show them the beauty of this life born to her from her encounter with Promethea—

her best friendliest friends were still a bit hesitant in a friendly way and best as always and slightly intimidated a bit discreetly and in a friendly way at the entrance, registering the very slightest bit of uneasiness,

—and H was saying: isn't my life beautiful? Don't you think it is noble and humble and proud like a life of Parsifal, was saying that with the naïvete of a child—but she is not a child, nor am I, being still always only a woman in the eyes of the Law and in the eyes of EveryMan.

And saying that with the no-naïvete of a woman of 1982, yes saying that with the masculine and the feminine proudly rubbing shoulders like in some Welsh adventure, taking each other's measure and finding each other marvelously equal in strength, number, knowledge, lyricism, in delicate ignorance and in loyalties, but therefore saying it with anachronistic recklessness—because we are no longer horsing around in 1182, H is not unaware of this, and it is without naïvete but with her ancient obstinate hope that she did her thing. Because of her trust, her stubbornness, because of loving Promethea, loving Parsifal, loving all the tales that are always freer than men.

To turn a single comparison into double praise. Remonstrating all paternal fathers. Acknowledging all maternal beings of every generation who guarantee with their very blood as forfeit, the stubborn candor—cultural hardiness—the spiritual and grammatical elevation, the illumination and the intensity of passion of their wards. To the memory of those unknown Brahmins or midwives, the wise women or wise fools who were able to explain the Proverbs of Freedom to novices at life, despite the din of tanks of planes of rumbling boots of raging voices in the press of every part of every country of every sort of every version of human stricture.

H therefore was celebrating. Like a little girl with her first poetic creation; like me with my first daughter.

And then, finally, it was my oldest, most faithful, and most gallant Him himself who ended by suddenly after three hundred silences telling her:

—"It's strange, very fine, very beautiful, but I don't really know quite how to say it, it is too woman, this present. It stays distant from me. And I feel there are moments when I am not there, when I can't follow. And yet in this place—or at least as far as I can see from its entrance—there is a hymn to woman that . . ."

And yet He stayed at the entrance. He did not come in. He said: "I feel the beginnings of a closed structure . . ." And H said to him: "Come. Don't you want to come? What you feel is not something closed. Come, I am going to show you where you can get through. There's the way. Through love." But He was very nice. Did not budge. Did not leave. That was when H did something naively unwisely naive. She said: "You love women too!" Nothing happened. But He, usually not a laugher, suddenly gave a loud laugh. H laughed too. And she felt a slight quaking. But then the air was abruptly shut off, the earth stopped, and she was upset when He said: "But my desire for women never takes this feminist form."

"Feminist!" H exclaimed, feeling like she was swallowing a prickly pear, peel and all. Her scraped throat kept her from answering. Those little thorns had to come out.

I hurry because I am keeping Promethea waiting. She is inside the book and working along on it almost without me. Several times already she has come to call me. The treasure is piling up. And I am still in the third chamber ridding myself of this last fear. I cannot do it any faster.

I am afraid because of how close I came to not writing. And even worse: how close I come every day to not writing. I am afraid of fire. I stole a glowing coal. And I do not know how I could live if it went out. I use it daily to make my dawn. Sometimes I live at a low flame, sometimes a roaring fire. In both instances I am afraid of extinction. I am the sort of person who is threatened by cold.

And what if Promethea does not like my plateful of fire? I want to give it to her. I want you to taste it; eat my fire, Promethea. (But if I imagine the face she makes I immediately imagine how I will sink into the icy abyss.)

OK. Here I go.

—How should I behave toward our book?

Promethea suggested I consult her Chinese Almanac of Passions, which has recipes for wisdom and for cooking. You are supposed to open it at random. There is an answer. I open it to . . .

I know a woman—for whom H has an even more chivalrous and fabulous passion than the one she feels for Parsifal. It is Clarice, the Brazilian saint of writing. One day Clarice wanted to tell another woman's life in a book, a woman who was really, absolutely other than herself. Because Clarice was a writer the other had to be illiterate. One can tell by the smallness of the heroine how tall this Saint is. She wanted to think of a person who could not let herself be surrounded, spanned, encompassed, or read easily by her.

She wanted to love a woman who would not let herself be seduced. Neither by Clarice's elegance, nor by her charm when she was gay and when she was serious, nor by her mysterious, venerable beauty. This woman would be so unconscious of her own existence that she never even felt she was visible, and she goes through the streets softly humming like a female gnat.

She wanted to deal with the most insignificant person in the city, because she was also the most important person in all the city, being a woman whose only reason for living was that she had received a life to live at her birth, and nothing else; and since because she held onto it and often said secretly to herself: "What luck that I, someone who is of so little consequence, am the owner of a life." So Clarice said to herself: this is the only woman who can teach me what I am incapable of knowing from my too high vantage point, from my memory, my treasure of images, my cupboards and my jewels and my four fountainpens and my typewriter, this is the one who can lead me into the primitive cave. And Clarice chose this woman to be her oblivious angel, to guide her toward the hell she so desired, a pathetic female gnat whose name was Macabea, someone slightly shabby, with not much hair because she lacked vitamins, with sores itching her genitals—which was only herpes and not even caught in lovemaking, but caught the way, in some lives, one catches things one does not deserve.

And therefore, she chose a woman because of love: because what she wanted to tell was the most pathetic and purest love story. Such a pure story that absolutely nothing else would be in it other than unrefined love, tiny flecks of gold at the bottom of the darkest rivulet; and at the bottom of the most forsaken caves, women, of course, are the ones who guard the marvelous flame.

So this Clarice, who made no mistake in her choice of angel—well, to write the story of this woman Macabea, she had to pretend to be a male author, yes, an author shaving himself, etc.; she felt obliged to do this as if she were afraid of frightening her little gnat if she had not looked like a man, a doctor, a postal inspector, or a policeman. But why? I wonder why?

And I wonder, was it so she would not scare the little gnat away? Because naturally the little gnat thought that it was always men who took an interest in a woman, even one whose nails were not manicured. Or was it really because otherwise she herself would not have been brave enough to go up so close to her, even if it were necessary to go all the way inside her, into her guts—especially because tiny women who are so skinny do a lot of their thinking with their intestines and their womb and their ovaries and everything inside—and then, was she afraid of being afraid of going in, of not knowing how to go in if she was just a woman . . . ?

Promethea, my beautiful luck, I love you. I do not want to justify myself. I do not want to disguise myself. I do not want to explain love. There is luck. I want to sing of it.

Some people, who shall be nameless, are surprised at the friendship between Clarice and Abd al Rahman. She who is (Jewish) and he who is not, he who is just and she who just is, and he who, particularly right now and she who when the tanks, and also since the last war, and moreover ever since memories began, and yet, with tanks camps newspapers crimes mirages, sexes, religions, disbeliefs, scars, debts, citadels, prudence, examples, the inevitable? necessary? natural divisions, the order of the world, the harmonious opposition of races, union for disunion, just now more than ever and still nothing yet. Some people were surprised in a friendly way, on both sides, both banks, both sexes. Then she thought about the last walk she took with Abd al Rahman beside the sea. She said: "We are innocent." She thought about the sea washing the soldiers' feet. "Innocent." She repeated. Nonetheless, to speak about the little gnat she preferred becoming masculine. That is something I will not do.

But I admit: I have put off arriving in the book, because my personal guilt causes me such anguish, and because I am at odds with Promethea. If there are any complaints I, the undersigned author, am the only one involved, the only one guilty.

We are innocent women. For Promethea we are. Therefore there is no use in saying it. It cannot be proven. She is right.

I like that better. Innocence is Promethea's style. We are

innocent. That is all I have to say. I know, it was a long time coming. I would have liked to begin our book with this phrase but was afraid that by exposing it like this to the first glance I might alter the transparency of our innocence.

But I also would have liked to begin with the trembling page that I let my hand dash off:

"I see myself opening your door

"I see myself opening your breast . . ."

Or by the real first page of the first notebook:

Here I am now. And it is hell. Paradise? Yes, I still am here, but who? only myself, with my small waist, my small soul, my small arms, my small intelligence pushed to its greatest heights and thus ruthlessly able to see itself shut up inside its supple transparent but oh ruthlessly inflexible membrane, if I push it any farther it will burst its envelope, I am going to lose part of my mind, we will no longer steer clear of madness.

There, here I am, nothing but me, me this nothing tossed into the sumptuous breast so infinitely alive I am swimming, everything crushes me down and lifts me up, I am going to endure a hundred thousand deaths by jealousy, my god, make me have the strength to survive a hundred thousand deaths of the wonder that is unbearable for someone of my minimal dimensions, make me have enough strength to endlessly endure being, because that is what I wanted, myself, this nothing but me, wide awake and lost in the midst of this abyss of glories, make me have the strength to stay awake and suffer, to stay and suffer and reach the heights of pleasure beyond the limits of my strength.

Give me the strength to undergo such superhuman bliss.

One of them says: your heart beats for my life. If you forget to love me for a tenth of a second my life would be instantly obliterated like a dream.

Everything that happens in our book has a pure violence. Everything, at least, is just being born or else dying. We cannot open a door without taking someone's breath away. To live burns—ashes' peace never. We roll around in fire like buffalo in the golden mud of the Ganges. Promethea's body when she comes out of my belly in the morning is coated with a layer of golden sticky velvet. I lick her all over. The Ganges tastes like sugary ginger.

Often one wants to die before the final hour.

Then, we present ourselves together to this final hour. Because in a book like ours the final hour is treated like a priestess, like a secret room, like a wedding.

One of us says, One way or another you'll be my death.

Sometimes to live so is murder. One would like to do more dying. I mean—to live more, more and more.

Already I have said that this is Promethea's book. It comes to me from her and I want it to return to her. Alone, however, I would never succeed. (Which is why I am asking for help from H; and even sometimes, humbly, from my own daughter.) Because something is there between this book and myself that makes approaching it almost impossible for me. A ring of fire that I am terrified of crossing lies between paradise and myself. However, we all know the acrobat leaps unharmed through flaming hoops. He is so lively and so nimble, livelier than fire. But the fire is livelier than I. It is so beautiful. Sometimes I am tempted to stop in it. To let myself catch. This very moment I have just passed rather slowly through a burning page. I am scorched and I smell trouble.

This book can kill me. I am not spontaneous enough. I stop, I turn around. Instead of leaping in with whinnies of joy, I start counting sparks: I mean—I slow down to listen to the words crackling in my heart; that is why I groan in pain. There is nothing to be done: I am incapable of simply enjoying fire. I want to understand its tongue, I want to grasp its words, I want to put them in my mouth, suck on them and pronounce them. I am crazy: I want to translate fire into songs and be the one to feed it myself; but I am consumed! I have to call H, or A, to help me die down slightly.

Suddenly this is not the same life at all: as if, wide and patient, I had been flowing in my bed toward death for forty-five years, when here she is descending upon me from the top of her mountain, she falls with all her force as if the mountain itself had turned into water, and she falls into my life one Monday in February, with all her sparkling waves to push my soul over my own banks and make me flood . . .

As if I had lived my life naturally by night until I was forty-five, from the first night until yesterday. I had lived my night until then, neither foreseeing nor hoping nor desiring any end to it, since I was blind; as if I had naturally been living my dark frozen life until last night, when suddenly it was the last night. Suddenly, rather than the next night the first day came. Suddenly I no longer come from a dark world. Suddenly, already, I am not at all of my world. Just one sudden day and forty-five years of night are so foreign, I was from that other world I know but do not know how to remember it, this morning the day is so brilliant that I cannot imagine night. How could it have been so cold, so enclosed, so naturally black yesterday? I scarcely remember, I am no longer part of that night, and yet can feel that I am not native to this day. Here I am in it, forever trembling with surprise. Yes, the unexpected day caught me. Fire! I belong to it. But I do not dare think it is mine yet. Never did I hope for it. That is why its coming feels so violent. It comes over me. I have burst into happiness, vertigo, and light. But I, now I want to take the fire in my hands myself, I want to caress my body myself, I want to begin to hope for and desire the day that surprised me, I want to go meet the world that has suddenly come upon me.

Wait. I close my eyes. Let me go cold again, let me remember the night, let me rediscover yesterday a bit, a bit nothing, a bit of the world where I was alone, let me invent some bit of time to engage in a little hope. Let me want and want again what happened to me. Otherwise I shall never be able to write Promethea's book.

It is a book too hard for the person I once was. Everything has become hard for me. I am living now beyond my power, I have to conquer every moment of my life, which has become immense and free and wild, and altogether new. This life, I do not know how to live it. No one taught me. No one told me about its turbulence. I think I thought "loving" was the sweetest, easiest thing in the world. Which is not at all what it is. No one told me about storms, squally winds on the edge of the abyss, eclipses of the sun, thirst that kills within inches of a spring. Never could I have imagined the terrors there are in joys. Wanting to scream for mercy. Joy is unbearable. And I never suspected it. I am exhausted. What happiness!

Promethea, you hurt me! I want to tear you from my breast, dear heart! Do not let me succeed, because I would die! Dig your claws in here and don't let me go!

How strange, this word Promethea—turned into a word of my blood.

You change everything, of course. The world's proportions are no longer the same as yesterday because you are its new standard. But I? I am strange to myself. I am unknown to myself. I am uncomfortable with myself. I also surprise myself myself. That is because one changes self more slowly than one changes worlds. That night I suddenly understood that I had to change every part of my being, not merely turn my gaze in the direction of a new world and discover it, but one by one I had to replace each of my old organs. Starting with my hands. I have ordered new hands, to caress you and to write you, hands that will fit you. I expect them soon.

The pages closest to my heart are the ones that hurt me most to write. "Be the eagle!" I ask Promethea. And she does. "Dig in!" I say. And she does. She plays eagle in my breast, and I press on her head, I encourage her, I push her until I feel her beak find the exact spot where this little pain nerve that began to quiver this morning—when I was unsuspecting—is rooted. What pain! I did not know such pain existed either. The world of pains is populous as a Tibetan Sangsara. And I have no lama. I have no Bardo Tödol. I have no shield no guide no book of wisdom to defend myself. The world of pain exists deep inside me and I do not know how to govern its people.

I am prey to insurrection. Who rebels there? My own nerves. My soul is tyrannized by things that are nothing and by everything. My soul too, I'll have to change.

This book is going to cost me flesh and tears, but that is nothing compared with love.

I did not know that loving brings so much suffering, and that even so one never has enough of this suffering. You make me thirsty, Promethea, my river, you make me eternally thirsty, my water. As if I had spent my life in an old house of dried mud, so dry myself that I could not even thirst for thirst, until yesterday. And suddenly yesterday, the dusty floor of my old house burst open and while I was still dozing away my parched existence, drop by drop I heard the music of coolness awaken the thirst under my dry soul. And leaning over the dark shaft of my life, I saw my childhood springs unearthed. Is that always how (by accident) we rediscover Magdalenian riches?

All I know: I could only encounter you, my oasis, coming out of a desert. Deserted myself. This is all right. My futureless and solitary self. When suddenly I hear the voice of springs—Right away you made me want to sing. To cry. Then to drink. But after the desert, the merest trickle of water sounds like a storm. And ever since, Promethea's every murmur shakes my life like an earthquake. I was asleep. I was not thirsty. It would have been possible for me not to hear the first three tears. Ever since I never sleep. I listen.

All I do is write the rain. Promethea is the rain.

Oh you, my deviner

You, my bringer of thirst and water

You, bringer of you,

You, the sudden, unpredictable giver

You who sang that night, you poured cool words on my dusty ground:

"I love you with all my corneous parts, with each nail and each hair of my body and each hair of my head,

"I love you with all my liquids, all my many-colored bloods, my sweat and my urine, my mucus, my saliva . . ."

You who washed my crackled memory, who moistened my dry thought with the wildest, coolest, wettest, words alive inside your Lascaux cave

You, who do not know you know how to sing

You, whose effect is like rain on an emaciated tribe.

All the water that is in our book, the Amazon, the Ganges, the seas, everything running between the walls and between the dust covers of our book, was brought to this earth by Promethea.

And yet, she is also the source of fire.

And I? I drink, I burn, I gather dreams.

And sometimes I tell a story. Because Promethea asks me for a bowl of words before she goes to sleep.

I do not know how to make things up. I only know a few stories. The stories that I can tell are love stories. I have already told them all. I tell Promethea the story of Gilgamesh and Enkidou, I weep a bit, I make a few mistakes, because for us they both have changed somewhat, they have rounder breasts but their fate does not change, their strength becomes weakness, we are unsuccessful at ignoring death. Enkidou falls ill and I cannot help him up again, tears flow from Gilgamesh's eyes and I say: "The gods frighten me, Promethea. Why have they let us off? And now, what if they condemn us?" And I look at Promethea as if I had lost her, I watch her from some time after, not daring to budge for fear she might vanish; I would like to say to her: "bite me, bite my belly, so my flesh will make me feel you exist in flesh and teeth" but I dare not stir my voice. Promethea listens to my tale and then my silence, her tears run down my cheeks and I feel better. I can open my mouth. "I don't want to tell any more love stories. Because all the ones I know shut the door that joy came in by, and I don't know any others."

Now I just want to tell a true story, one not made up. It is our story, our history. It is us. This story could be called "Our Luck." Sometimes we tell ourselves how it began and we frighten ourselves. It came so close to not beginning. And even now, where there should be a beginning it falters, goes back and forth, hurtles on, disappears. We do not agree. It escapes us. It took us by surprise. But we did not perceive it at the same moment. Our story is two different stories and yet their waters are equally sparkling and turbulent, they run along for ages, each in its own landscape, and it seemed to us they would end up pouring into two seas that were very far apart. Then the earth quakes and Promethea foams from her bed and falls torrentially, with all her roiling waters, into my then lazy current.

So this is a story that almost did not happen. Pieces of luck wove it a cradle among the reeds.

I once thought I was Moses. But Promethea is far more Moses than I. By luck I found her left for the birds on the banks of a river, by luck I was taking a walk precisely that day and not some other, by luck I spent that winter in the region, that winter and not some other season. By another piece of luck no one was in my house that day, no other day, and by another piece of luck there was milk and a fire. There was a lot of luck that went into our chance to begin this story. But so much adverse fortune too. I did not want to. And Promethea did not want to. And then there was a will that rose in great sweet squalls and blew and pushed and pushed us with an intoxicating roar around our heads. And, finally, Promethea was the one who felt that there was something starting to be told her, but I heard nothing then except a sort of melancholy song. That is why we think this story might have been another story, one I would not have known how to tell, and only Promethea would sadly have known how to sing it, but not to me then; and then we tremble.

I am afraid of luck.

To continue:

And then? Then I did not want to. With all my being I wanted not to want to. Then, Promethea, it was my violent silent luck to see you come out of the bathroom and suddenly, violently, my rescued child, I did not want you, and it was luck that I did not want you just at that instant and no other, so violently, that it was as if an angry, burning will shouted: "go away! I want. I don't want. I don't want. Go away. Please leave. Go. I want. You to go. My will is immense!" But I did not open my mouth. I was the only one with the key to this luck: you had no key. Promethea, you do not have it. I saw you come out of the luckroom. I saw you. You stood in the doorway. I violently wanted, I resented you. I resented every detail of you. I did not spare you. I unwanted you. You did not know, you had no key. Only just tonight am I giving it to you. It is the key to my strangeness. The key of luck. I do not know which is the right or wrong direction to turn it. You were wearing a bathrobe, I saw that. I did not see your body. I did not look at it, I did not try to see it. I did not try. I did not see the color of your eyes. I did not see your face. I saw your feet, my god! My violent luck was to see your feet and I was afraid. And immediately I was afraid again because I had no key to this fear. I saw your bare feet. I saw the nakedness of your feet. I saw the nakedness of your soul. My feet were armed, my soul hidden behind my great shield of ruby silk, my shield of invisibility, and I saw your peaceful feet. In my hand I held my little Atlantine book, in which I am able to read formulas for fighting at a distance, with no spear or sword or bludgeon to pierce slice club with magic spells pronounced, in my hand my little book of magic hostilities for saving my skin from the enemy at a distance, my little book of the well-defended not-allowed woman. The moment I saw your feet I opened it, the moment I noticed their terrific radiance, and yet, my Bradamante, I did not know, I was unaware, I was far from guessing, all I was sure of was my book, nothing else. I thought I was seeing your feet, but already I saw your soul, I did not know it but my soul guessed it, my soul behind its ruby silk shivered in fear, my soul recognized you, not I. I thought I saw you come out of the bathroom, which was in fact the whole truth. I thought I met you in the doorway, which was entirely true. But my soul already saw the other truth. But my soul saw only the present truth. The future truth not even my soul foresaw. When I wanted to read the spear formula in my magic book, the radiance of your feet kept me from it. You were not the one who attacked me. Your feet were peaceful and luminous like the faces of babies. The glow of this very peace engaged me in enchanted battle. But I myself I did not know, I facing you, I facing the door to the bathroom, I in full armor, I no longer able to read my own book, I no longer able to think my own thoughts, my eyes were struck by the light of your two feet, and that was the simple truth, the simplest, the most unthinkable. With your feet you stopped me from reading, you were far from suspecting this, I suspect. I did nothing, you did not run at me with a spear, you challenged me neither with looks nor with gestures. Your innocence, Promethea, was what flashed this dreadful light into my eyes, and I had no defense against it. My book was powerless. The hall was so narrow. I could not run away from you. If I stayed there facing you, it was not out of courage but out of fear, that is the truth—fear of seeing and fear of being seen. But my soul already saw the other truth. Only my soul can tell the story that began in this doorway, slightly to the left of my gaze. There is no other witness. My soul alone saw the struggle. Like lionesses, like eagles, like sacred heifers they bellow, mutate, slip away, shatter door frames, grab each other, go all out to win, clutch, confront each other until fury is assuaged until anger is quieted, until denial is exhausted, until love is allowed to triumph. My soul alone saw the allusion.

But I, facing you, only felt my strength becoming weakness. Suddenly I was tired. My heart full of blood with a strange, bitter taste, I thought: "you are someone born far from the city, who, tomorrow, will be able to go back to your reed-lined bed, and I will return to this book of mine for which I need to keep my eyes' strength." At that point, because of the nakedness of your feet, and because of my own need for shoes, books, a shield, our history almost did not happen, but through another bit of luck—equally blind but visionary as well—this history reappeared where I did not expect it and because, this is really true, I did not expect it.

If I had understood the allusion. If I had known that that day, five thousand years ago, we were entering Mesopotamia. I was wrong about which book it was, luckily, I thought I recognized Ariosto's style. Perhaps this mistake is what saved us. All my weapons were useless, too modern, unsuited. Did I make an honest mistake? Or a deceitful mistake? I will never know.

I thought you were Bradamante, Promethea, my betrothed these five thousand years, but I wonder whether I should blame myself or be glad I did. I wrestled all wrong. That's certainly what happened. While my telling blows aimed off at illusory skies you made tea, today's not at all imaginary Earl Grey. Which is the most magical thing of all, my today friend. Not making a big to-do, making tea.

And then?

Then there is one now after another. There is no big to-do, no story to describe, what happens to us is magical time whose source and whose heroine is Promethea. Promethea says H is bewitching and I say that Promethea is heroic: it is perfectly clear where we are coming from, how far apart our civilizations are.

Right now, on this very page, I have just discovered what I would like to write someday (it is perhaps too soon this time because I am just beginning, so slowly beginning, to change civilizations). I want to write The Imitation of Promethea.

Why, this Friday at 3:30 in the afternoon do I think that? Here is the situation: all I have done today is think about Promethea because she isn't there. When she isn't there I "think about" her in various ways: sometimes I conjure her up, I see her, I show myself long slow imaginary movies, magnifying things to a mammoth scale so I can observe her very, very close up. Then it is like having my moon on the tip of my telescope. I see every pore, every mountain, every ravine, every inflection of her voice, and I take note. Sometimes I tail her: I follow her (mentally) wherever she goes, whatever she does, I watch her a way I never see her in reality, I imagine how she is in my absence. (What I see is that, in my absence, she is a faithful likeness of herself, she resembles herself, the only clear difference is that her whole being is in stronger and less subtle colors because of the hordes of eyes illuminating her. Her whole being is "louder," more resounding, like her voice. But she is essentially the same, it is as if one could see down through ordinary shoes and there would be her bare feet calmly standing on the ground, on the earth over which with no power, no kingdom, no violence, she rules.)

(But today I am aware that I am not getting her right, yes, in spite of myself I keep coming very close without seeing her, I drift badly, I disobey myself, I lean out the window of my memory, I do not see her in reality, I see her in an unfamiliar dream from which I cannot awaken. It is because of this sea between us. The earth has never, up to now, separated us. But, ever since yesterday, there has been something in this nonetheless real, perfectly Atlantic, salty, slightly rough sea that has cast an evil spell on me. And every time I think about Promethea, I see her crossing this great expanse by boat and soon, alas, a storm comes up, my memory clouds over, in a flash there are shipwrecks, I cannot even cry out, my mouth is full of saltwater sobs. I am flooded with vague, deceptive recollections, I am drowning my imagination in tears borrowed from the most familiar tragedies, I wish I had never read certain books whose poison is working in me. Has this Friday, perhaps, thrown a spell on me? But spells only work if you catch them. I have caught the Tragic illness. If only Promethea could make me some tea I know I would find relief. But that is exactly what is impossible. And so, today, I am sinning.

I am sinking beneath reality. I am weighted down with literature. That is my fate. Yet I had the presence of mind to start this parenthesis, the only healthy moment in these damp, feverish hours.

All this to try to come back to the surface of our book. And imagine how much Promethea hates my little floods of fantasy. If she only knew!

If you knew, Promethea! sometimes I wait for you at the exact edge of the jetty where we left each other. Sometimes I disappear into an unconscious hole and lie there silted up in stories having nothing to do with the vigorous immediacy of our epic.

Phone me quickly, Promethea, get me out of this parenthesis fast!)

Our history has a bumpy geography:

It happens on the edges. It began on an edge of life. Everything starts with death. We live on the verge of dying. Which is why we are breathless: each breath is such an explosion of joy. Sometimes when Promethea wakes up in the morning she cries, "Hallelujah!" Because she has just been given the world. Sometimes I wake up in the morning before Promethea does, so I can see her take the world. Her exhilaration entering the day! A new visit every day. We'll never be done with visiting life. Often I look back, trembling with fear that death or jealousy is about to catch up with us. I see that human beings, women especially, have no right to enjoy divine bliss. I look behind the door, behind the clouds, I am afraid of planes from hell; aren't I jealous myself, always jealous of myself?

But Promethea knows nothing of jealousy. She just believes in God.

It is as if we were living at the edge of the abyss at Les Baux. We fall asleep there, right on the brink of the blooming, aromatic cliffs, we cling to each other's embrace, with just a bit of heather between us and nothing. There one of us dreams of hell and the other dreams of paradise, I might fall, you might fall. I am not afraid. Why am I not afraid? Because even an abyss would not separate us . . .

If you slipped, how could I catch you? You are so heavy, my throbbing boulder, that if you slipped I would slip with you to our death.

Each holds the other's life in her arms. A child out over an abyss. A crystal vase delicate as a bubble in your hands, my heart is iridescent in your fingers.

We each tremble with terror, and trust.

One of us asks:

—Carry me, hold me out over the chasm, I am trembling, make me afraid, make me tremble, make me shiver trusting and terrified.

—I want you to tremble, I want you to be afraid, there is nothing to be afraid of, I only want to have given you everything, I want to save you from the abyss, I want to snatch you from the shadows. Fall, dear heart! At the last second I want to gather you up from your other existence, and into the first second of the life I want to give you; what can I do to bring you into the world, I want to be the womb that bears you, my mother, my child, I want to drop you in the night, I want to snatch you from night, my day.

Sometimes spasms of desperate wrath shake our history:

because when the hands of one tremble just a little, the idea that one of us might drop the other shoots through our heart (and then we have only one heart, one is inside the other, one is the other, each of us is herself, terror, the other, the arrow, the scream tearing through one another's womb).

It is extremely hard for us not to hurt ourselves: our heart is like the heart of Siamese twins. But it is also extremely hard for one of us knowingly to hurt the other a little because we are made in common.

I would like to say one last thing about our history. Because I have to use the right words to talk about it, but perhaps I am going to give the wrong impression: I say, death, blood, violence, trembling. And Promethea's book is fire and fury. But is that not the very climate of happiness? And about happiness: in the world of our encounter the temperature is always capricious, varying naturally according to our emotions, especially mine, which fluctuate wildly whenever Promethea leaves my magnetic field. It gets very hot, very cold, the earth has mild convulsions, only the sea stays calm; but the light especially takes on an odd intensity: if I get ready to embrace Promethea—and every time it is as if I were embracing the world, it is simpler and simpler and more and more religious, because from that moment on rarely does the kiss remain one between the two of us; it is scarcely given before it calls the whole universe to celebrate, in an infinitesimal and incredible celebration, genesis fills the air we breathe—so I have scarcely bent to kiss her before I see the earth quiver, the oak tree three steps to the right of Promethea suddenly lights up, all the leaves catch, and the tree goes deep into my soul with Promethea's eyes forever. Yes, the whole world is stricken with my amazements. Thousands of ecstasies come over it. I had heard about this. Now I have seen it.

To get back to your feet, Promethea, at first it was a sublime disgust I felt toward them, understand? I had no idea what my terror meant. Your appalling, heavenly feet floored me. But my soul knew. My soul saw that one day, if one more day were to follow the lucky day, one day, I would bathe your feet, which are like children, I would caress your feet, which are like women's hands, I would feel this sublime appetite I feel today.

At the beginning there were a number of struggles, in the hallway, and outside the bathroom, and in the small, enclosed chamber of my heart. A struggle for, a struggle against, a struggle for yes, a struggle for no, a struggle to spit it out, a struggle to swallow, a struggle to refuse to refuse. Never, my angel, have I felt such an immense spiritual repulsion. And ever since: hunting, harrying, I track you down, run away, I hunt your soul in every corner of your body, I hunt without weapons, it is a love hunt, I turn clever and powerful doves loose on you. But this is not always possible. Sometimes where you hide is inside me, I have to search myself to drive you out of hiding.

And that is the cause of our drama. The book opening behind this page is the journal of that drama. Our drama is that we live in a state of mutual invasion.

Which is why we do not even know who is the reason for this book. For me, the closest to the pen, well-placed, I think, to decide: it is Promethea. Consequently: everything that follows has moved through my hand and onto the paper when there was real contact with Promethea. I have often put my left hand between her breasts and with the rapid motions of my docile right hand it was written. I am only that cardiograph.

But sometimes my left hand is overcome with joy, and without even noticing, I go completely into the hollow of my own hand and the paper no longer hears a word.

The most beautiful things cannot be written, unfortunately. Fortunately. We would have to be able to write with our eyes, with wild eyes, with the tears of our eyes, with the frenzy of a gaze, with the skin of our hands.

Where our history moves out into the sea today it is so beautiful, I must be quiet. The things that happen are too beautiful to be written.

I remember the blessed moment when we were face to face. Then the blessed moment when we were side by side. Delicious closeness. Love at my flanks. It was good. Side by side we went through a forest, our two souls lay deliciously at their ease, each of us easy in her heart. Then slowly you sank into me, you made your way into the city. I no longer know which one it was, we went in through the streets as if there were only one body, I claim mine was the body taken, Promethea swears she was invaded, where can we be, where are we,

now you are in my breast, says one of us, you are planting yourself, you are pushing up, you are growing, you push my heart, you are supplanting it,

now I only remember the time when you were only outside of me. What was that like again?

Now you are not only outside me but also within me. I am full of you and empty of you. How can that be possible?

If I am ever to get to Promethea's book I have to make up my mind to pull my right hand out of here. Wait one more minute.

One last line: Promethea's book is a rough draft. It is made up of two notebooks. I will not touch this draft, because it is pure blood and sometimes one can hear drop by drop the hot singing of its song, sometimes it is raw blood that spurts.

Something more to add: the feelings expressed in the two notebooks as I see them today (I am reading these winter pages on a summer Saturday) seem to me a bit green—a bit timid. I am glad but it also worries me: I do not want them taken for our words now. Obviously, this is the problem with any book when it becomes read. But as far as our book is concerned, the problem is all the more acute because it was written in this drop by drop of our blood's time. In the dark at first. Then in the wee hours of the morning, then in broad daylight. With this line, it is now after midday in our life. Please take note. We are no longer in the first notebook. For example, in the winter notebook you can see how I have to deny Promethea the very thing that in the second notebook I have an equally strong need to give.

So many of the soul's impulses have a different value now, a different meaning and so a different name. I owe it to us to be clear: thus, I used to call what I now call generosity, dependency, and I thought it was bad. It is not my way of thinking that has turned upside down, it is my life which has suddenly turned toward death and smiled at it. Now that I am going in the direction of death with Promethea, I think of it (death) altogether differently. I have far more respect for it. I do not forget it. I offer magnificent sacrifices to it as a sign of gratitude. My dread of death is better than ever. It is truly odd that my thanks for this is an increase of vital resources: I live full blast; the doors are open. I hear cascades of blood thundering down the walls of my huge heart. I have become immensely bigger than myself; I am burning beyond my means. Moreover, never have I had the hearth of my soul draw in so close around its sole blazing crucible. Twenty times a day I think I will die of a bursting heart. Yes, I cannot conceal this, we drive ourselves from tenderness to rage until we are out of life, and every sweetness rages more mysteriously. We never die enough, we keep on getting sick from these inflammations of the soul; Promethea, especially, breaks her body and comes all apart, because the wildness of her soul is even more energetic than the wildness of mine; and she throws herself around inside herself, against her own walls, with enough violence to break bones. She has already cracked a vertebra; she fell down the stairs several times until she finally broke her ankle.

What seemed reckless to me yesterday, things I see I still

disapproved of in the first notebook, now seem timid to me. Things I would have condemned in the name of caution, proper limits and temperance, delight me. When Promethea tells me: "I want to be your slave," it doesn't frighten me, I don't reproach her for wanting to give up her most precious possession, I do not secretly worry about words that are dangerous for their author and for myself, I do not blush at hearing words that are out of date in these liberated times; all the suspicions I would have had in 1981, even up to where the second notebook begins, have been left behind: I understand the magnificent logic behind this madness. We have already given each other so much that what do we have left to give? Almost nothing. So now we give ourselves away. And when there is no more blood for me to give? Then my eyes. Yes, eyes next. Promethea has already asked me for them—not right now, we are not there yet. I still have blood and milk. But afterward. I said yes. And after my eyes? We shall see . . .

That is how it is. A lot of feelings I would almost have been ashamed of last winter today make me almost proud. Or at least at peace.

For example?

For example our cannibalistic tendencies. I remember my state of mind last winter when I told Promethea, "you can go, I won't keep you," not even pretending my detachment, because I have always been a wonderfully well-mannered woman. Good breeding made me dexterous. I used tweezers, forks, gloves, shoes, crutches, fans, stilts, every sort of tool for keeping a distance. If there had been toothgloves, I would have had them! I remember how distinguished I was, and I laugh. I remember how stupefied I was to see Promethea not hide her hands, not protect her eyes, not add makeup to her lips or her words. I remember my politeness, my disapproval, my circumspection, my confusion, when I saw her take on a strange land with no weapons, no helmet, no protection other than confidence; her hair bare with a hundred curls anyone could grab, her face exposed, her nondefense, her nonprotection. And oh, more magically armed with your disarmament than any weapon ever. I became your transparent armor, Promethea, I am your skin, your silk, your steel. But sometimes I turn against you and eat bits of you. I remember that winter there were immense territories between us, also populations, societies, people great and small, children, furniture, cars, associations and cities and memoranda, not even counting my closets full of helmets and coats of mail, and the fifty thousand volumes of my great wall of China.

And you naked.

How could I defend myself?

How in the end could I defend myself from smelling the fragrance of your flesh?

I sneezed, I spit, I caught a cold and then my lungs were congested; for weeks I resisted and in the end I smelt it.

Which makes me think. Are there any walls stronger than a fragrance?

And cannibalism? Once one begins to smell it, putting the apple in one's mouth doesn't take long.

Of course, when it is a woman the movement is very slow but eventually there is no god who can keep us from tasting. And then . . . Afterward, there is still this agonizing heavenly hunger, a torment and feast in itself.

There are moments when we keep hunger a little distance from our flesh, like when we go to the market, exchanging one hunger for another. Some people go to the market the way one goes to war or to a soccer game, to beat everyone else. But Promethea goes as if she were attending the baptism of all life's children. What felicitation! All the mothers of vegetables and fruits smile at her because they are so happy to see a human being who cares about their progeny. The mothers of the fish, who take on aggressors with horrible sharp knives in hands plastered with scales, spouting poisonous stinking curses against them, welcome her like the knight destined to lift evil spells and they turn back into cheery fishwives who know everything about the land and sea there is to know. All the deep things forgotten from the beginnings, from the time they were seeded, suddenly are remembered at her hand. Life's story is pieced back together. Things turned loose and dispersed are brought back together, religions are revived, we are given back our seasons, thousands of magical herbs are saved, once again the secret of growth is passed on, everything gets back its color and its speech, tomatoes breathe their understanding of how they reached maturity, up and down the ladder of production we go, from the marriage of earth and sun to the presentation in the temple, and on every level thousands of desires, attentions, astral forces, gestures of love, are brought back together, every instant the chorus creating life is miraculously yet not miraculously in tune, yes, everywhere beauty and inevitability sparkle, and Promethea discovers garden cucumbers and ancient rites, and the whole market suddenly takes on the brilliance of a Shakespearean comedy.

That is why sometimes I want to go to the market the same way I want to reread *Les Illuminations*. Or the same way I want to see a dream of a Hindu palace, which rarely happens to me. In the market things to eat are so alive, so meaningful, so eloquent and young, that one starts loving the things one will end up devouring. It is a love story that is both magic and absolutely real; it is our history. The story of love.

You are the market genie, Promethea! You are yourself the magic, unobtainable herb. I go to the market, I look everywhere for you, looking for an herb that makes the dumb speak again, and divulges the taste of love to victims of enchantment, to desperate people and to those who are forsaken.

At the market, when I go there with Promethea, thousands of little love stories no bigger than that take place. Last Saturday, for instance, I saw one lived out by a tiny old woman not far from death and a tall young man selling minuscule goat cheeses. It was beautiful: there were goats, a mountain, misfortunes, the hospital, big knotty arms, there was milk, a lot of the milk of human kindness and goats' milk too, and there were three little goat cheeses shaped like a heart as a token of their union. All this right in the middle of everybody, right before our eyes, and there was no doubt about it.

At the market I sleepwalk in a Persian tale told by Promethea. It is the tale of everybody, including the things they exchange, the tale of crude desires and delicate desires, and I too am told there. If I went to this market too often, I would write no longer, I would not practice my little pen profession. Who knows what form I would end up taking to hide in a stall, what skin or what feathers I would wear, waiting there for Promethea to come and choose me, deliver me, taste me, swallow me, absorb me the way I want to eat her, in bits as a matter of fact, well-spiced with the smiles and good wishes poured on her at the market.

But am I going to say that our cannibalism is a happy one? If there is such a thing as good cannibalism then ours is it: I insist on telling all the truth that is possible. I do not really want to eat Promethea the way Penthesilea was determined to eat Achilles. Love does that only when there is nothing left to lose. Then it devours itself. It is truly the only way to end this endless perdition. If one must lose, she feels, at least the loss does not vanish into infinity. This meal is the most wretched of all consolations. As for our cannibalism, it remains unfulfilled in reality because we have not been reduced to the grief of griefs. But it makes itself felt, very real indeed, in the stomach, in the esophagus, in the palate, because in terms of passion, that's where we are: at that untenable distance that threatens always to disappear. Keeping it is a matter of delicate balance: I almost fell into Promethea a few days ago, I went so far and so long into her waters that I almost was unable to reach my own shore. And then? I was terribly afraid of losing her. And I stayed out of her, drying off for two or three days.

But as for cannibalism? I will never have to eat Promethea

I think. But I know something through love that I can swear to: Promethea is the only person in my whole life that I would really like to eat. I love her so much that if I had to eat her someday, I know that I would think she was divinely good with every mouthful.

If I try imagining a mouthful of anyone else, naturally it makes my own soul vomit.

If I imagine a piece of Promethea in my mouth, even the worst piece, I don't faint, in that very second I imagine it, and I don't let go of my pen, I imagine the worst piece, and I gently chew with all my soul, and I love it, because I love you, Promethea, so much.

From that, one can gauge the distance covered since the first notebook. In the beginning we were still rather far from paradise. We could even think it was possible to retrace our steps. Now here we are: that is, there is no other path than the one drawing us always closer, deeper, more now and more forever.

I said that when we sleep on the brink of the abyss we dream of hell and of paradise. I would like to emphasize that it is there, on the edge of the world, that paradise begins. That is what makes me sometimes feel that I have arrived at love's real hell—I speak for myself alone—because beyond the edge of the world everything must be created. Even the earth. Living alive in paradise requires superhuman (maybe even angelic) effort. The truth is that the process of arriving in paradise is pure paradise. Then if one wants to stay everyday one must accomplish the impossible again. No free apples these days. (But they are even more delicious, even more astounding, for being won.) We are not of the first paradise—the one that could only be lost. Here it is all to be won. What luck! What a catastrophe! It is a joy and backbreaking labor.

I want you, Promethea, fruit of my heart, I want you everyday. But some nights the day's gardening has been such toil that I don't want you anymore. Suddenly I am tired. For a whole hour, sometimes I don't want you anymore, I tell you to go to the devil with my forgetfulness, I throw myself along with you into this state for a whole hour, I de-exist, I renounce us, I do not live, I do not exist, I do not think, I act like someone else, for one hour but never longer. Because obviously I cannot remain much longer without a heart without blood without fire, without suffering without joy. Without wanting to die, desire, shout for being alive again.

Thus, when today I speak of paradise, I am thinking of the one that must be created with powers we do not have, ones we must invent; I think about the garden that must be created beyond the earth we know with earth we have to find. I think about the plants and forests that must not only be made to grow, but which we must be able to name, feed, and love. Because to make a paradise live, it must be endlessly thought about, willed again, every day it must be sprinkled with tears while we stroll through it with words of praise and encouragement. There is no paradise that can endure without a supply of everyday tender care.

Have I meandered? I'll come back. That was all to say that I think the first notebook is rather cautious and calm, pre-paradise. Then as we rise it grows stormier and stormier: that means we are approaching where the tide turns.

I would like Promethea's book to stay where it belongs, on its true page: therefore I feel obliged to leave it in its authentic, immediate state, disorganized and even dated (not taking into account my ex-taste for discretion in writing).

Rereading it is going to make me dizzy, impatient, and nostalgic. But also it will astonish me that I was hit by happiness, me-why-me, me in fact me, why so suddenly so late so inevitably singled out, aimed at, hit and staggered. And now the agony.

What comes next starts out as an underground river.

What comes next is the current of a passion.

At its source I did not think it would overflow the well where it was born. It was like a little lake of tears. I thought I could drain it. Could I have foreseen that it would become wilder deeper and more virginally desirable than the Amazon? More fertile in legends than the Nile?

I don't know. I foresaw nothing. Today we are so broad that it is hard for me to remember the first trickle.

It is impossible to go against the current in what comes next.

We are going toward the sea.

I have swollen. I am carried away.

Sometimes at night love comes up so quickly and so high, and if we have no little boat perhaps it is because we want to roll breathless under the ocean floor. But not always. Sometimes we just want to die great, sometimes I want to die a little less quickly because I want the time to reread our agony. Sometimes I beg: "I want to go under again! Drown me!" I dive into the cave, I thread my way among viscera, I want to catch the heart. Suddenly I am caught. My own heart is hooked. I scream in exasperation, "You are too much for me!" I am on the tip of heartrending desire. I want to harpoon you. I want to be a harpoon. I want you to be my whale, I want you to be the sea, swallow me up, let me swim in your guts and then spew me out. It is as if I were a fish and I wondered: "How can I be too much for the sea? How can I drown the sea?"

Sometimes our whirlpools and our whirlwinds so coincide that since neither could lash the other to the earth, and neither could weigh down the one who was floating up and unable to hold herself down, one inside the other we rolled into the abyss which was sky maybe, sea maybe, head over heels love, neither one nor the other able to want (even in order to be saved) to part with the other's breast; entwined we flow spinning beneath the great silver blades of time, eternally until one of us wants to watch us die.

Sometimes this is a window thin as a sheet of paper. From either side we watch each other, the silence of a smile separates us and we see that we exist.

Sometimes this is a burning bush. Crouching by the fire I

contemplate it and adore it until it gives in and calls me. Then I move up, I slide between its burning breasts, I suckle the flames. I cry: "Softer! Harder!" I blow on my own pyre.

I say: "Don't burn me too fast! I want to taste every spark." She says: "Don't come. Don't come in. Stay out of here, away from me, don't move. Do that, do it, please, exactly the opposite of what I want, I want, I want you to dare to do."

We confer:

—Should I change the order of the notes in the notebooks? Because it starts out with such convulsions.

—Don't change anything.

Even if it seems to start out badly.

—It starts out worse. But it is the book of changes: it all turns into gold afterward.

—What shall we call it?

—Right now it is sometimes called "Promethea Unbound" sometimes "Promethea Booked" sometimes "Promethea delivered." It is Promethea's book, it delivers a pound of Promethea.

—You can take away my food. You can cut me up in bits and eat me, you know that?

—I know that. I've already done it some. I just wrote that.

One of us adds:

—This is the strangest book I've ever read. This is a book of raw flesh. If I had wanted to write this I never could have written it.

—I did not want to. That is why it came completely naked. Nobody looked.

I let it go by in front of me. But afterward I am the one who will write.

—Shall we permit ourselves just one departure? I would rather move the first pages of the first notebook. Promethea prefers to be merciless.

We leave it up to the toss of a coin.

Permission granted! What luck! There are gods too.

I swear that this will be the only exception, unless unintentional, by mistake.

Our book emerged like a birth-cry, after a night of silent savagery. I noted it (this night), with drops of blood, sweat, and urine, before everything dries I remember I noted it, trembling, in hiding, behind Promethea's back, to forget, to not forget, to distance savagery.

Because in love not all is love . . .

. . . A silent attack. Because the Enclosure slept so pregnant deep and peaceful a sleep. Because She was so far away in sleep. This one woke a she-wolf. Love woke her up. Still sleeping while the she-wolf was awake? The sun woke her up. And she in the depths of peace, immured in innocent walls of peace. And She vast and murmuring as if she herself were night.

While the she-wolf prowled. Wide awake. Famished. Was already on her way up the sky. And she, like a night innocent of its own end, was sleeping.

And the she-wolf already way up and facing the vastly innocent dark night. And her stretching out—limitless and trusting with no memory yes with no memory, and hanging back farther and farther vastly farther and farther in the strange immediate distance that started right there beside her.

Day's desire: to pluck out one of its rays and stick it in night's silky back.

Contrary angels battle above Her. About her fate: I shall beat you with my love, I shall tear you apart, I shall make your blood spurt out for sleeping far from my lips. I shall make you feather armor and a shield of magic words with my love.

Why?

Because you are too close. Go away. I have to leave.

But the moment you leave, the moment you take some distance, the least distance, I have to pursue you, I have to catch you again.

The very least distance and the gash in my heart becomes immediately as wide as Wild Woman Ravine.

You cause me every possible pain. And every pain is happiness. The bitterness you filter into my blood is so sweet. Poison me. (Before going . . . help me sharpen my arrows.)

The one who is awake thinks:

Never am I you. That is what is astonishing. That is what is reassuring. That is what is too much for my love. I lick your soul right down to the bone, I know the taste of every inch of your nerves, but you I do not know you I do not know.

. . . . .

There is a blank page. Then the notes begin again. During the blank page, Promethea woke up screaming: "Help! She's leaving!"

I am copying this over because tears washed out the first draft:

The one who is awake thinks: "We have to leave each other." Strikes the defenseless great night in her naked back with pointed, transparent thoughts.

Thinks: "because we are so close

because we are so far apart

leave each other, separate Us . . ."

Until the one asleep utters a horrible cry: "Help!" And rolls onto her belly stirring up tons of water and raises twelve-foot waves, and falls back moaning onto the day's rocky bottom and scrapes her back on the ridges, letting all the tears accumulated by dreams come down in torrents.

The dream narrative: She did not dream it. She felt it plunge into the flesh of her back like a harpoon; while she smiled and slept.

Because in love not all is love.

But also: injustice, anger, hunger, delicate hunger and raging hunger, innocent hungers and cruel hungers proud of being so and ashamed of being so and even prouder.

A need to place my body in front of yours to fend off the spears, a need to wound you, to plunge a blade into your adored belly while shrieking in pain and needing also to be the spear myself, jealousy of the spear, and a need also to wound to satisfy the need to heal . . .

Because in love not all is love.

All the tenderness and kindnesses were my jewels and my armor

The days when love was for me a matter of art

I was a sublime acrobat. I trained my soul to do dangerous tricks. It knew how to fly through flaming hoops like a dove. It knew how to make its face bloom serenely with a virginal smile while I was swallowing a sword soaked in acid. How much I had learned!

—And now? I'm civilized no more.

Stripped of my jewels,

I have flung myself naked into the night dying of fear that I will be unlucky and once and for all break all my bones and all my souls. Dying of desire to fall as luckily as an escaping star falling for a long time at a crazy speed and whistling in the intoxicating darkness of night back to the breast of the sea,

like the angel at the top of the ladder who madly merrily dives into ever-blacker erotic darkness ever brighter ever sweeter and becomes a silver-feathered arrow and wants to end up embedded in the heart of the volcano it came from.

(Because Jonah's real story is the one never told: never was he as stupendously happy as during those three days and three nights of eternity. He was granted an experience that women dream of: he lived when he was mature in the adored whale's belly.

In real paradise.

How does one get there? By disobedience. By passion. Running away.)

There was no child there yesterday. Today it is born: it has forever entered the flesh of your life. Its life is added to your life. Its life is forever part of your life.

The absolute violence: this child is not a child, it is a woman.

With absolute innocence absolutely innocent guilt, we let ourselves move slowly toward a fatal bottomless happiness.

—Since when? Love?

—I don't know. I don't know. Before loving you.

I loved you in the darkness at the center of light.

The fire at first caught sweetly violently deep in the marrow.

This began in darkness, in the depths.

The fire spread. Suddenly the heart. Caught fire. This blaze hurt.

Rung by rung descended into the breast's dark red, descended toward beginnings toward the savage heart drunk on its own blood.

Day by day climbed up into the deep light of pure madness, grew higher and higher taller and taller more flickering more trembling saw everything burn brighter and brighter, were more fiery more burning.

I am describing you to me, I am describing desire: I would like to touch the insides of your heart with my fingers. I want to touch desire with my fingers. I touch you, I seek you, I can tell it is you, I forget you? I forget you, never.

Terrible agonies they cause each other because they have no skin. Naked organs. Badly burnt by love. Each word makes them scream.

All that could slip through their clenched teeth: "You have it."

With her fathomless eyes she said: "Is it what you wanted?"

She meant: "Do you want my heart between your teeth? You have it.

Do you want my head in your belly?

You have it."

Everything she wanted to tell her, was unable to tell her, because she was afraid of hearing her own voice come out of her heart and be covered with blood, and then she poured all her blood into these syllables, and she offered it to her to drink like this: "You have it."

(And not one drop kept for me.)

Everything she was unable to tell her because, in her effort to pour out her feelings, she could only keep half a breath, which was, "You have it."

You wanted your footsteps on my soul's ground

You wanted to catch me unawares, while I was expecting you from the east you wanted to come upon me, on my west?

You wanted me to rise and walk straight toward you without looking to the right or the left or in front of me

She wanted to say to her: "Is that what you wanted? Well, that is what you got."

Rather than that the other one, her head like a rising sun, said: "What I wanted . . ." With her sunbeams that rose and fell around her face, and that fell for a long time onto the ground onto the body stretched out on the ground onto the face nakedly exposed to the face of the sun—"What I wanted," she said, with a voice that came from her throat like rays too, she said, "What I wanted—was," she said, taking a long time to choose a word from her quiver, "what I wanted," a word with a heavy shaft and a point sharp as a needle, she chose, and leaning over the earth which was murmuring "Is that what you wanted?" she let the word fall dead center onto the other's breast, she said: "What I wanted was that you be smitten," and the word fell dead center onto the other's breast, she was smitten, a word so keen and so charged, which took a long, long time to plunge dead center through the breast toward the heart and, finally, touched it, finally found the heart and there slowly buried itself, blade into soul.

—I did not see what was going on up there, I had the sun in my eyes and my eyes slowly filled with dark tears, I felt though what was going on way down deep, it was the deepest slowest and steadiest pain, which plunged slowly through my breast toward my heart, it was a long piercing hard sweet pain that bore down on me and advanced ineluctably toward my heart, it was a pain called *dor*, which plunged deeper and deeper like a caress until it reached the heart, and like a caress it was desirable, she desired it, she did not beg it to stop she wanted it deep in her heart, because there only, once life has been run through, once the heart is finally touched, once the heart is finally pierced, there only would the pain begin to calm and settle down, in the end, at the dire end. The fire has to burn.

And afterward:

—I didn't believe you, but the word was so charged and so cutting, it pierced my breast like truth. You gave me a taste for dying.

—You wanted to die?

—I didn't need to die. I was dying.

Haggadah

—Why (you know everything) do I want so badly to hurt you?

—Why, while you are asleep, do I suddenly want to waken you by rending your breast with long slow stabs.

—Why do I suddenly want to see death slowly fill your eyes with its silent tears?

—You who know everything, why?

—I know words to make you die, they are words that would make me die.

—Why do I have this heartrending desire to make agony's shadow cross your face?

—Why do I have this desire to gaze at you seeing you lost in thorn woods.

—Don't call me. I won't answer anymore. Call me, so I can not answer.

—It is no room that you enter.

It is my breast, you enter and go straight into my life now, already so much farther than I.

So now, how are you going to get out of the room? You can't. And I can't let you leave it. How could I let my heart leave?

—And they went for each other, go away, leave, go away, get away from me, leave, I want to leave, I want you to leave but how can I let my heart out of my breast without dying, without your dying?

—What is happening? whispered a burning breath in Promethea's throat. The breath burned everything it passed all the way down into her breast.

—This is what's happening: together we are descending the stairs of the heart, which lead to the sources. (It is a secret staircase. I knew it existed. Which is why I avoided it. Because it leads to the other-life, deep, underground, the fluvial, the painful.)

We are in the process of descending into the depths of the heart. To where bodies communicate with each other.

Was in her arms on her breast. What happened: bit by bit felt that Promethea's blood was running through her own heart, and turbulently, feverishly, was trying to mix itself at her breast and that was what inflamed her veins, this invasion of foreign blood that made all her flesh throb with pain, and set her lungs ablaze, and churned her guts. Because the mixture of all this blood was violent, blood to blood, and that was what bewitched her.

—You enter me through my skin, pore by pore, perfusing every feature you come into me.

How does your face come into me? every line passes onto my face, every line and its history, from the first look, and enters, your upper lip sometimes swollen with emotion and slightly raised like the lip of a watchful bitch, enters. My heart beats in your mouth, but my breast is giddy and deserted. Your mouth enters sometimes pulled tight between the two deep lines of a tragic mask and I weep.

You are Beauty, the Beautiful. You are Beauty, the sublime, the whywithall, You are young Alps, mountains still shivering as they come out of the sea.

It is a matter of possession.

You reach my depths. Wholly. You, whole, all the way to my body's guts and all the way to my soul's guts, that is how it is. You come and I let you. I cannot not let you come into me, with your whole big warm presence, and slowly you come into the bay, under full sail and filling me from one shore to the other, you are going to anchor in the depths of my belly. Enter slowly! not too fast, enter sailing the way a dream comes toward you with all its sails full of wind, and slowly fills the belly of reality.

I cannot not let you fill me. It is just a matter of impossibles between us.

A case of possession goes like this: you give me the desire to possess you. No. To be more precise: you do not give me, but your being, your body, your shape, your breathing, awake in me a silent desire hidden up to now among familiar desires, a desire that had no hope of ever being awakened during the course of my history. This is the desire you speak to.

And here it comes with a leap and a flame, it is a warlike desire, yes a very ancient desire, it is a young warrior who once upon a time had to go to sleep, a desire dating from the time of the Nibelungs, noble and terrifying, joyous and fierce, a frightening desire to take you, I who have never taken, never wanted to take, who takes nothing takes nobody, I see a young and proud desire rising, a desire to bring you down, to embrace you, to measure your size with my arms of flame,

(I am laughing: I recognize this one, it is a Homeric desire—from the period when friendship was love and enmity had all of friendship's graces.)

This is how I want you: larger and smaller stronger and weaker taller and trembling more, more out of breath than I more burning more penetrating bolder bossier more yielding more frightened narrower and more relentless than you are more than I.

The more deeply more tenderly to turn you over into me my heartrending child, the better to fall into you when I am overturned.

No? no one knew me? No one ever knew me? I didn't even know myself. Only now am I making my acquaintance. This is exactly what I was afraid of. This is exactly the woman I advised myself never to risk being.

It is exactly this voluntary impatience and this involuntary patience. It is exactly this decision that I never took that is taking me.

A treasure: I have thousands of pictures in my treasure chest:

The way she runs up the stairs, comes in, her head haloed in its own radiance, cries: "I told everything," frightened, runs up breathless to tell, delighted, is seven years old, runs back down, frightened delighted crying, "I told everything."

Violent strange moments: suddenly I suspect you of bad

character, egoism, sadism, childishness. Immediately on the defensive against the way you shine, I unmask you, I strip the skin from your face, where is the truth where is the truth, I am afraid of you, I beseech you, show me your real face, this one is too beautiful, show me the ugly one.

You who cry you who laugh the way you cry you who spout you who snort and quiver, who stamp and shake your great silver mane, you who warble, you who spill your liquids and sweat honey!

One of my most precious scenes. A pale pearl. It happened one evening when I said:

—I washed your socks and underwear.

And it was as if I had branded her breast with a red-hot iron. She cried out: "No!" She writhes in confusion. Beats her forehead on the ground. Moaned. "I had hidden them!"

That was true. I knew that.

—I wanted to do the most intimate thing I could. I wanted to wash your socks.

It was a gesture of the greatest love. I knew you had hidden them, out of love, I looked for them, I secretly stole them from your secret. Out of love, out of love's indiscretion. And now you stiffen and roll around in pain as if I had burned your right breast, my Amazon. And this, no doubt, is what I wanted to do?

—Don't turn yourself into a pack of crazed bitches: I would turn myself into a bird and disappear forever. I will leave the earth behind for you. I will have fled it.

—You overwhelm me with reality.

I believed you did not exist, my dream.

But you are coming true now, with all your weight. Lie heavy on me, my dream. Spread your limbs out over the entire surface of my life.

—The things you are ashamed of! And I love them all. I

love your shame at not knowing, and I love your shame at knowing, you who are supposed not to know. I love your shame at never having time: to wash your blouses; to wash my blouses; to immediately circle the world at a gallop with your mistress on your back; to read every book; to build a little temple by hand at the back of the garden . . .

Day and night, constantly erupting, the child Titania floats on her vast maternal rivers

She comes from mythologies. Still all aquiver from being born. She rolls over on me, her new bed, the last one, she murmurs between my reeds: "my mire, my sacred mire."

I saw you, huge heavy-thighed statue, three thousand years ago in Crete, at dawn, your gaze carved out of night by the coming day, your mouth drawn out of silence by a brilliant smile, I saw you recumbent but alive, dreaming at the edge of wakening's brilliance, a very naked goddess.

I heard the sound of sobbing in your breast, sobs of wonder, because what a birth it is to awaken! You inhabit a primitive castle, lined with blood satin. An archaic statue with a powerful body, that has scarcely come out of the earth, with legs still so earthly, with colossal legs, with a broad, majestic neck, but whose head already partakes of the world of great birds.

I and my bloods, we want to come into your castle, we want to stay in every room, every corner, lick every stone.

—Because, your eyes sparkling glances about to go out, you are asking me:

—Will you still want me next year?

—I want you every day and I want you every night. Forget what I just told you.

—Forget it? How? When it goes so indelibly deep down inside me?

—Forget. So that one day I can tell you again for the first time: "I want you every night and every day I want you."

—Forget. I want you to ask me next year once again for the first time: "Will you still want me next year?"

—Why do you love me?
—Because, your throat distorts your voice when you say, "Why do you love me?"
Because even if I did not love you, you love me.

The way she arrives: last minute. Last breath. The way she comes to breathe her last and revive on my lips.

The way she arrives after having run since the beginning of time. Her eyes weeping from the last things she saw. Her eyes naked as her lips.

Through the forests galloping. The magical mare on the path. At my door. Suddenly silence. From the other side of the door. Is she waiting for me to turn my head toward the door? She hears my silence through the door. She sees my head turn, the door is closed, she sees through wood. Then, now, my gaze is turned toward you, expected, unexpected, you can come in.

She enters, her whole body shaking. Her mane soaked with sweat. I am dripping too, my blood boils, my heart, losing its balance, cries out.

(—Do you want some tea?) (Or something else?)

(—I want your life. All I want is your life, nothing else. I want every drop of you. I want every thought. I want to drink your soul. Give me your soul to drink.)

Felt sweetness raging as they gazed at each other. Eyes dilated, tensed, gazed at and desired each other, wanted to be torn from their lids, how painful to be only eyes!

Once again:

You are born to me, once again, this week; you are born to me entirely different, all kindness and youth and soft white silk hair; you are born to me entirely happy, free of shadows and not a single tear, barefoot through parks and palaces as if conceived from some fantastic, loving tale by the great magic mare with her mane of oriflammes. This morning was the first time you left paradise.

But the last time you were born to me as heedless and rambunctious as three thoughtless youths, rashly and absentmindedly mean, and several times that week I cried. You hurt me, you left me between two sentences without even noticing, you left between two words, you galloped right out the window while I was talking to you, you hardly listened to me, climbed to the top of a yew tree, you did not even hurt me on purpose, you wounded me with innocence, without offense or desire, and more than once that week I hated you I wondered what misfortune ever conceived you.

From all sides you are born to me. And every time I immediately adopt you. I have already adopted you twenty times, more quickly than I liked. Yes, you are born to me, whenever you feel like it, and already, immediately, you start going back and forth barefoot all the way down to the velvety depths of my house where I myself have never set foot.

I feel your steps trample my absolutely virgin flesh.

That is the way it is: you come to me. I am already thoroughly inhabited by you.

Violence reigns: everything is violence. Every gesture, every phrase, every smile, is a surprise attack; we are driven, beaten, tormented, by everything.

Don't open your gaze so wide for me. I am going to fling myself out of this gaze.

Violence: everything is sweetness.

When you said to me: "We have to defrost this refrigerator," I cried out as if you had hurt my feelings. Because you really did hurt my feelings that instant when your mouth should have uttered only my names.

You collapsed against the door at the moment in which

who knows what gaze left my eyes in spite of me and hit your neck.

She did not tell her:

—If you want me to jump out the window I'll do it.

She did not tell her:

—Open up my breast, carve me up and take my heart.

She did not tell her:

—It hurts so much, I want to kill you.

I want you to sink your arrow into my throat. And the next instant I want to slit your throat. I don't understand myself.

She did not tell her:

—My heart is too small to hold so much love. That is why the fire spills everywhere, I have fire in my breast, I have it in my shoulders, I love you with the hollow of my neck, I feel fire in my knees and even in my ankles.

All that one of them did not say: all that one of them would have liked to say. All that one of them dared say. All she would say . . .

Like nobody. Like the model for Terra Incognita that Michelangelo saw in a dream. She comes from the deepest night. She takes off her huge dark blue sweater and it is day: broad sweet daylight and bigger than life.

Fear? Vigilance. Because there is such endless outpouring.

I am raining. I weep my blood onto you. I am afraid that one day I will no longer have a single tear.

I am raining. My wetness is passionate. I foam. The seas are all on edge, under your weight the seas curve and crash, the seas want to drown you.

I rain down thousands of words that never sipped air before.

You are the reason, this earth makes me quake.

Today. I do not want to talk anymore. I want to regain my silence.

Today I shall not mention my love to you. I am going to

forget you. Fly right over you. I am not going to touch you. I shall not know who you are.

I want to shake you off. Seeding. I first need silent earth.

I fear gods the way you fear bad dogs. I am afraid they will jump on me and tear me apart.

Because humans are not allowed to be so happy, they are not allowed to be larger than themselves, they are not allowed to go and live radiantly on the shores of death.

Humans are not allowed to be awake and healthy when they enter the gardens on high. I am afraid the gods will shoot at us. I am afraid they will roll rocks down on us.

I fear the gods. I fear they exist. I also fear they don't exist. Because if they don't exist who is going to stop me if I go too high? Who if I scream too loud will shut me up? Who if I love too hot will chill me? Who will save me from the Too Much I must surrender to, and must escape.

I notice that there is often a "she" in the first notebook. I did not remember having to use the third person so often. But now, in a now-distant memory, I remember, back then, how strange I was to myself: I went beyond myself so suddenly, I yanked myself away, I was carried away, I was no longer the one I was before, back then; I don't know if I was yielding to or resisting that one. It was all so intoxicating, so fast. At that speed even fear gets caught up and becomes a kind of intoxication. I was so afraid of going too fast, at the mare's gallop, a kind of vertigo spreads throughout one's body, undoes all the tethers, one no longer knows if one is moving like a flash of fire toward death or toward life, but one can only go all the way there in the other's breath. While I hang onto the mare's neck, my soul down inside my dissipating body, disoriented, is falling either up or down, but the mare knows where she is going.

Next in the first notebook I see how I was trying to rein her in but I could not find a bridle.

I was dying of fear we would reach the end, in paradise.

But at that speed fear turned into desire.

That was when I finally said the last word. It was a word I had promised myself to save for "the end."

I did not want to say it, I did not want to say it, I did not want to say it.

There was this fateful week in which everything turned upside down. And I too turned upside down, curled up inside my carapace, I let my self roll over and over right to the edge of the earth, not knowing until the very last minute what would come out of my shell.

(*First notebook*)

What happened this week:

The rise. Madness rose.

The irresistible impetus to exhaust, to combust.

As if the demon of love, the one she had banished moreover, the monster, the *pregnant enemy*, had suddenly returned despite her orders, intruding, had come back through the labyrinth, the monster that says, "as I am a woman as I am a man," if I am one and if I am the other, both together will I devour you, we will sweetly overcome you, if I am a man I am going to knock you down into the green grass with a glance, and if I am a woman I shall press down on your breast with love's unmerciful sharpness, I, she or I, will plunge my cruel arrow into your melting flesh, easy as cutting bloody butter will I go into your breast and you will not even feel it. All you will feel is a bitter languishing, all you will feel is a dull pain, you will feel terrible sadness for no reason at all in your soul; in astonishment you will feel your blood leave you, leave you your faithless forces, faithful forces oozing out.

This week: The turnaround. Crazy times are already here.

She began by doing everything she did not want to do. That began Monday morning with the arrival of huge happiness its flanks aglow, whinnying with a tenderness that was impossible to hear without fainting dead away, with its silvery mane of foam; she followed it without deciding to, immediately, into the forest, at a gallop—one gallop—because stretched out on the mare's neck she herself turned into the hot quivering of this joy, and immediately in one racing torrent, far from the house, far from the city, far from reason, in one breath, dashing hoofs, heaving flanks, whirlwind breath, shouting, nothing held back, no brakes, no concern for decency, forgetting the conventions, shouting in joyful terror, they plunged in one flaming leap into the heavy fragrance of the forest's heart. Instead of going to the university to give her course.

And what else did she do? That she didn't want to do? The worst thing. (Even worse than that:)

Invisibly left the earthly plane farther and farther behind. Let her soul plunge into the faraway heights of happiness, where air smells so good, so good, smells of love's flesh and love's blood, where the air is so intoxicating, smells of the breath from love's lips, and where if one does not struggle (with the help of State and family gods) against oneself, if the police do not come to the aid of the drunk, one can linger a whole lifetime breathing, just breathing and inhaling the scent of happiness, yes, she can remain in drunken levitation, transformed into a transparent bird fluttering slowly before love's dawn-colored lips, her wings taut with desire, her eyes half-closed, hovering level with the deity's great musical lips. Musical? Silently musical.

(From her lips the full infinite sound of sacred syllables arises, sound they do not utter, but that they promise, that they delineate, like a reminder of eternity's secret name.

They softly imprint on the air: "I love you," so softly that the air does not stir. As if they shaped God's name with silence.)

Intoxicating the soul and fluttering in forgetful and selfish happiness. Going off in broad daylight, in the midst of social gatherings, in the middle of colleagues' conversations, in the middle of discussions with her own children, to drug herself with love, to get drunk on god.

And then, the world seen from the brink of love's immense lips, is a silent film, the world is the dream of a lazy dreamer beginning and drifting off, scenes vanishing in the middle of a sentence, scenes that end in another world, in another too-distant time, in another dream.

And then? she is ashamed that she has let herself be drawn so close to the day's lips so far from the world, she is ashamed, that is all she still has to offer the world—frightened shame, that's all.

Even worse:

Not having enough personal misery anymore to be able to savor with sincerity the bitter misery humans share.

So then how could she really suffer from the misery in Salvador with her soul so enflamed with happiness? Couldn't feel cold. Forced herself to suffer, did so badly, remorsefully, absolutely remorselessly.

And even worse. Her personal worst. The dangerous worst:

Began to burn her boats. Betray her promises: because she had sworn (to whom? to her reason?) (but not to her madness) not to go into the forest without carefully anchoring at least one little emergency sailboat. At least six. At least one.

Had sworn not to run ahead. Not to go beyond. Not to hurry on. Not to tap her reserves. Of what? Of time, of present, of past.

All the things she did not want:

To change her rhythm of life.

To change the floor her soul lived on. The soul's landscape. The view out the window.

To change economies. Hairstyle. Makeup.

To change her tastes, her stubbornness. Her dreams.

She did not want—

To stop not believing and not to believe. In the possibility of love, of victory of loyalty of presence of respect of delicacy between two creatures of the same species whose strength is equal. To stop being sensible about not trusting, not hoping, not asking, not doubting that there is no other one for her—there will be no other, no other.

She who did not want—

To renounce her peace; the happiness of finally having become the desert, the contentment of a dune in the sun; the triumph of renunciation; did not want to renounce renouncing; at the moment in which she had just made solitude her fiancée; to renounce the endless, barely rippled, bright, dry happiness of not being unhappy. All she did not want to do, with good reason, with every reason and no madness at all, everything she had learned from having soared and having crashed, from being broken and getting back up and soaring again.

To renounce the rare delight of restraint.

Began by permitting herself a few moments that gave a hint.

She who did not want

To run barefoot down the tower to meet the other. Wanted no longer.

To cross the world from west to east no matter how to spend an hour with the other, and the crossing lasts an anguished horrid month, plus thirty days of customs and mountains and ravines and the crossing rips skin from her hands and feet, and lasts thirty nights of nightmares and battles with the dragon, but at the end an hour lasts a lifetime with rustling brooks, orange trees in love, pomegranite trees full of nightingales. No longer wanted to take the first airplane to the other.

To cut one by one all hundred strings holding the soul in its place in society, hastily swiftly to cut the strings and turn the soul loose in the sky's blaze, and the soul takes off straight for its beloved star. Did not want to let go of solid ground, the solid city, the solid day, and shoot off toward a vague night toward a strange star, one, perhaps, already cold.

Began to fly without knowing if there would be any wings for her up there.

But her personal worst, was that she began expending words. By the handful.

What she did not want to say. She said it.

It began with little names of endearment.

Soon they were big ones.

Began by feeling her blood gush.

Felt vampired. Tell me, tell me. Did not want to tell, did not want to say any more. But her mouth opened, words came out; that too was what she wanted, for the words she did not want to say to bubble up inside her and burn her throat.

Did not say. Blood shouted by itself.

Bled. One evening bled so much that she knew she was going to faint soon. That is what happened: glistening red sentences spurted. Soon she no longer knew herself what was coming out. The sense was bright red and that was all she knew. Maybe the sentences were saying insane things? Did not know. Was not hearing herself.

Had just time enough to hear herself murmur "bad poem" before sinking into the depths of a dream full of fiery shivers.

And afterward it all happened somewhere above her whether she agreed or not, it all did without her. Her love was squandering her, in abundance, wherever it raged.

Everything she never would have said (precisely because of her concern with respecting accepted limits, and not offending good taste), love said it—immodestly, immediately, inconsiderately, in . . .

Love said: " . . . "

(The words must not be repeated. Besides, people have their own secrets. They lose their force when revealed. These are unique words and she let love chance them.)

Was ashamed and fearful. Thought love was running deadly risks.

Right up until she finally, suddenly, foresaw that it was

going to do something very, very serious; was going to say the last word.

The word she had kept back, the lone, most terrible, most dangerous word, the sacred word, the most fragile. The one she had promised herself never to say before her final breath. The one she wanted to keep true, exempt from any test of reality, the one she was not supposed to say before the last day of her life, because otherwise it would, perhaps, not be true in the end, or it would be less beautiful, a little worn out, old,

the word she wanted to keep young and far away from time, from events, that she wanted to keep silent and sleeping, and would not awaken till the end,

suddenly foresaw that love was going to shout it, now, as on the last day.

And then tried to prevent it.

There was a very short fight because love was far heavier than she and had no trouble at all knocking her down. She lost love won. But where was the victory? the defeat?

Then love announced: "I have something to tell you."

And with no further ado said: . . .

But, going through her lips through her ear to her brain and her marrow, the word's wind almost killed them. Because it was so charged with energy. Like an atomic word. They trembled.

And afterward? It was too late.

Wanted to shout: don't listen! But it was too late.

It was all over. It was said.

—I'll never tell you that again ever ever, she swore to herself.

And swore not to break her word. And begged herself to respect her oath. Perhaps if she obeyed herself for twenty years, perhaps then the word would be returned to her, still young and virginal and she could say it once again for the first time? And then it would be the only time, the first and the last.

Destroyed?

(Or else) is there yet another word beyond the last word?

Now had to begin learning dispossession.

Dispossessing herself of all her reserves. Did that with a sort of wild—maybe sacred?—intoxication.

This way: closed behind her all the secret ways out: now she could only go forward, forward.

Like this: closed, sealed every opening onto the past.

Doing so passionately: nothing from yesterday was to have a present, nothing that had taken place was to be preserved. Could not be. One lone present—unique and innocent and universal, the present of passion.

Was that wrong? It was cruel, ungrateful, unjust, immoral, incomprehensible, ruthless, immoderate, imprudent, pitiless. Verdicts came down like knife blades raining: has been; has been; has been.

A severing, tearless mourning reigned.

She herself was inspired by terror. Meanwhile no protest against the power of the new Reality: so powerful, so willingful, so fulfillingful that every decision had the sparkling purity of the events born of revolutions. Because obviously there was no hesitation—one could only have protested in the name of uncertainty.

Love reigned—one so strong that disputing it would have been senseless. It was absolute. Therefore absolutely innocent. Had no other law and no other memory than its own and they were young and absolutely free.

She would have wished, perhaps, to feel some regret or some nice familiar feeling of confusion, or a hint of guilt. None of that at all. There was no punishment. No reproach. It was proud and a little fierce inside the room.

One cannot bear to spend a Season in Paradise without crying out in instant nostalgia: never will we have the strength to endure such intoxicating agony a second time. If we had what we will never have—time to live this day over again—there are so many others desirable and each is the most beautiful one. It is superhuman torture. We do not know how, simply, to bear it. We weep for joy. But they are the real tears of sadness. We hang onto each other as delight and memory do: "hold me up!" "hold me in your memory," "I am dying, I want to die, don't forget me!" One dares not leave. Suppose the door were closed when we returned? One can only die trembling. It is so beautiful, this is such a sweet abyss, this face is a ravishing song, it celebrates in one instant with all its thousands of lines the fearsome miracles of love, one sees everything, the discovery, the delights, the threats, the victories, our entire epoch is truly painted alive on one single face, this sight is so tremendously beautiful, this beauty lifts us up, goes beyond us, what joy what pain, already what regret! Yes, there is much we regret, especially me. Never have I regretted as much. I feel I am not great enough, not fast enough, I feel my limits, I am enclosed in my little shell, I who believed myself open and vast and airy, am dry and wooden. Break me! Crack my shell, Promethea, my brain is a poor squirrel that some spell has shut up inside a hazelnut. It thinks and thinks about the hazelnut, about its smell, its taste, it thinks and thinks and doesn't eat or smell or taste anything. Oh, Promethea, you who know how to turn into little creatures or into big ones, depending on what you need, turn into a hatchet and split me open, here I am, here, on the table, in the bowl, where you put the fruits and flowers, here! don't you hear me? she doesn't hear me!

—(Finally she heard all my commotion. She came and opened the door for me. I had fallen under the spell of a very evil metaphor. She set me free. But I am still thrashed and crushed.)

—I go on: Because most of what I was trying to say is true.

It is a matter of our human inability to adapt to our own possibilities for growth. We go beyond ourselves with love's help. Sometimes we leap over our own limits and we land unhurt on the moss. But sometimes the leap is not magical enough, we have forgotten a word, a heartbeat, and we stay put with a heavy shudder. That is a bad sign: that means there is bad faith, unwillingness, and especially: separation. That means: go without me. Because sometimes there are unforeseen, often imperceptible, breaks in love. They can last about as long as a thought or a bad dream; they can slip by unnoticed and without injury. But if such a break happens in the midst of a leap, then something that is only space with no gravity suddenly can deepen into an abyss.

But it is a matter also of how difficult it normally is for us to bear the infinite. Nothing would distress us more than continual happiness, other than the discovery that our much cherished happiness would eventually suffer from not being threatened. We are made for fragments of eternity cut to our size. We need day and night. We need to die to be born. We are creatures for recreating and recreating. Our constant recreation is what is at stake. What I wanted to tell is how Promethea and I respond to this ordeal of paradise. I drift endlessly because it is such a beautiful morning that I have trouble imagining rain. That is the way it always is. Transitions have to be sudden. Anyhow, Promethea plans around suddennesses for her stay in paradise. She always lives there as if she always has and always will. Whereas, I am never able to forget hell.

But sometimes Promethea will succumb without warning. Suddenly. In the space between two seconds. A step away, on an errand, or sometimes I shut my eyes or turn my head and she has vanished, really. I shut my eyes, I open my eyes, and it is still dark! I see the day but this night is there inside the day; my soul is stricken with night. Promethea is no longer here, not in me, nor in herself. Then I think she is dying, then I beg her, I give her three seconds to return, otherwise I shall never again be able to look at her or take her back into my bosom, then she still is not back and I hate her, yes, a quick hatred already busily makes itself known and begins to turn out the lights in every room, then I silently warn her: that if she keeps on abandoning me I am going to abandon her, that I already don't love her any more than I hate her, that I already think she is too dead and cold, I who love her fiery, that she is killing me, that I will be dead when she gets back, even deader than she is, then I begin to be cold and to die, slowly, then faster—and afterward—afterward it took us tropical hours to warm our lips up again. The last time, moreover, I was so frozen that even after regaining paradise I had stubborn little icicles inside my guts for several days.

That is how Promethea deals with what is unbearable about our season. She disappears the way she comes, and she pops back up, heavenly and suddenly—the way she disappears. When it has been too beautiful a day, she stabs the sky in the belly and plunges suddenly into the gash with a flash of her peremptory mane. And I don't have time to see where she has disappeared. I expect to see her pop up almost anywhere, I am disoriented. How hotly I quarrel with her when she resurfaces, her head soaked with all my tears! I thought she had gone to Never-More. I do not celebrate her return. Or rather the great celebration is a furious one. I heap accusations upon her, oh, I treat her shamefully, I treat her to extremely harsh reproaches. Once I even managed to call her a monster. Even I was astounded. Never had I hoped to plunge my tongue so deeply into her soul.

I am unjust. I want Promethea to stay in the fire. I would like to forbid her ever to leave the blaze. I want to give her crazy orders and have her crazily and scrupulously execute them. But, personally, I do not want to die a cinder myself. My injustice is pure, unfair, conscious, involuntary. I am really unjust and I don't give a damn; am I not exercising one of love's prerogatives? Is love not the most marvelous injustice, the most charming, divine, joyful, and beloved injustice.

I have not told Promethea:

—I want to be your slave   your queen."

She, bareheaded, weaponless, without paper, without a mount, without a car, without a ship to sail, without a place to fall back, said that to me. It is a phrase that can only be said dismounted, standing, alone, before the walls of the world, open-faced, open-eyed, the soul facing death or life, with a legendary dauntlessness. (The same phrase said inside walls, or with eyes closed and the air full of domestic racket, would bring on immediate servility. But this one, naked, rude, and naive, has a lofty and ancient nobility.)

I have not yet been able to say these words. I am already on foot, I have kept neither horse nor boat, I have dispersed my troops, the phone is out, I am not having it repaired, I have no secret hiding place, I am not thinking of running away, but I have not yet said this phrase. I have not yet found the courage within me to bend my neck, I stand up very straight as usual, I am only a centimeter taller than Promethea, I prize that centimeter, I feel it, I feel it on myself, quivering proudly on top. All my worry and all my assurance have taken refuge in my paltry plume, all my strength is in my centimeter, I am only a little ashamed of it. I admit that on the grounds of nakedness I am defeated.

"I don't want to be your slave, Promethea, I am afraid I won't be beautiful enough at it, I am afraid I won't be big enough, have enough dignity or freedom for it, I am afraid of being mean and stingy, I am not yet big enough for humility, I am not yet ready for the descent that will attain the heights of paradise, I don't dare lower myself and become the earth, I am afraid to turn loose my throne and fly away, I would like to take flight, but I want to keep my trapeze, I am still too small in my bigness and too haughtily proud of my size to give up this one centimeter of my head. Obviously it was easy for me to strip away all my possessions, properties, human and symbolic props, in order to become light enough to be a candidate for paradise. I say 'easy,' but divestment is always easy, joyful, hasty, and a relief. Otherwise we could never get our clothes off our skin. I dumped it all. And no longer value any of it, except this thin centimeter."

That isn't even quite true. I know things about myself that I half dislike.

I never leave like that! I tell Promethea. I would never suddenly surprise you by disappearing. I have other ways of leaving, that's true. Besides, am I ever exactly in the middle of happiness? I try to stay in the center of paradise. But I planted a paper tree on the edge of its fig forest. While we are eating figs and I am watching a sweet anthem to these fruits that are so animal and so intelligent wash across Promethea's face, I keep an eye on my tree (which looks like a banana tree) and I am delighted to see that soon I will be able to use its leaves. Not the way you use fruit, not something of the moment. There are so many things one can do with the leaves other than eat them. One can write; make parasols; screens, fans, little huts, lots of things that are useful for adornment or shelter. Afterward I realize it is how I ward off the unbearable: I have brought paper into our garden, I use this ultralight gear of mine to deal with happiness. I always have some paper in the room right next to paradise. With it I make chairs, ladders, little boats, handkerchiefs, walls, sails. I have whatever it takes to go away, in a way different from Promethea's. I am even able to write her letters that are meaner or more naked than myself. When the waters rise I rise too, I have a flotilla anchored in my study. And on the days that Promethea wakes up three times bigger than I, my centimeter is useless, and I hurry to puff myself taller with a few long-winded incantations.

I do not know whether I write to stay as long as possible as close as possible to eternity or whether it is to rest from so much ardor, or to slip away in an eclipse less brutal than Promethea's.

Is this how I escape the blaze or how I keep it going? I don't know.

All I am doing here, anyhow, is putting down traces of Promethea. Only the paper is mine. The rest: light, movement, and breath, the fate of our book and of our adventure, is hers. The style is principally hers as well. I admit that sometimes I am afraid that it is scandalously naive. But upon rereading it I was very surprised: I think it has a modesty that I personally could never have invented.

The thing I would like to do: record Promethea's right-now, its mystery, the drastic nature of its pure violence.

Write along with the present? I am right there with it. In hot pursuit.

Write before it cools off? Before memory gets there, before it has begun its embalming and forgetting and storytelling.

Welcome its violent strangeness with another strangeness, also violent, its skin peeled away. I would like everything to be written as if Promethea wrote herself alive before me. Suppose there were no paper! I am afraid it muffles our laughter a bit, I hope our cry will tear it.

No rereading, scarcely jotting, quivering . . .

—A need to be as present as possible in the present. I want to marry you, encase your heart, embrace all your nerves. Be your skin.

And immediately after the present, right now, when the present still is there, has just left, has just gone into the next room, and this room still smells of juniper, it is still warm and echoing softly, and in the air there are still transparent echoes of its colors: fire and honey, honeyfire,

—Promethea is the astounding Present given me by God. I am astounded. I accept.

Just before forgetting, slightly before memory, yes, before the past begins to pick up what is left over,

I stop everything. I stop circulation, I hold my blood.

I lean my heart against the door of my breast.

And I listen.

Why? I want to put my head on the present's breast and hear her flesh murmuring.

I want to know the present as presently as possible.

I want to explore the vast transparent and immediate continent. There is a treasure so plentiful and so mobile that it is almost impossible for us to enjoy it. A treasure of events as sublime and brief as lightning—and me so slow—I want lightning to strike me, I want to take the lightning in my hands and contemplate it with a gaze deep as seven days.

I sing Necessity: the possibility almost impossibility of this gesture. It began with no plans, with no future, without my knowing it was beginning, what, something, the book of burning fires, it began with intolerable heart pains.

These were unfamiliar pains. (Now I know them so well, they are my frightening companions, my soul eaters, they chew on me and use me up and empty me, and fill me with their bites, their breath, their cruel, capricious, inconstant, constant appetite; I dread them, I dread their relentlessness but I dread just as much their sudden repletion, I want them to spare me, I don't want them to abandon me, I want them to abandon me long enough for my heart to get back its blood.) They have suddenly burst into frightened moans. Suddenly they have fallen shrieking onto my heart, they have dug their little claws into my heart, and they have begun rocking and moaning. I never knew such lively musical pains.

—That was Promethea writing at this moment directly on my heart.

I remember, I did not want to keep them, I did not want to accept them, I wanted to hide them from myself, scorn them, I told no one that they were there, I kept on smiling, even dead tired, after the first notebook, I was smiling, I counted on letting go of them, preserving my haughty self unchanged in my elegant heights until they were gone, I counted on discouraging them with my disapproval and my indifference until they vanished by themselves.

—No one had ever yet written on my heart.

And now I am the one asking: "Come in Promethea, please come in. Write yourself on me, I want you to cover my organs with your great signs of life."

The truth is, therefore, I am not writing: I am exposing myself to impressions as faithfully as I can. This takes guts. And organs that move fast. But above all the guts to go open-eyed where we go with our eyes closed, carried away into madness by Fury, the great invisible mare who carries us off some evenings if one of us says, despite ourselves, the one magic word, galloping, her mane swollen with storms, all the way through Reason to swirling frenzies. I owe it to us to write as exactly as possible for as long as I can hold my pen inside this frenzy, in the midst of all the racket, bravely until the terrifying scream that rips my diaphragm and

(but here I cannot continue—please excuse this page) we had such a violent apocalypse that night that I lost all my writing equipment in it, from the light at the end of the tunnel to the electricity in my nerves—which is too bad, I feel I could relate this incredible event—a one-of-a-kind event with its sins, its deaths, its hallucinations, its revelations (I can still see it all clearly, which proves it was not a dream, I see the wounds, the spears, the knives, the blows, hands armed and disarmed, I can pass back through inflamed viscera all the way to scraped hearts, back to causes, back to the first sulfurous glow, to the second just before the explosion, I feel it all, in fact I am still dying), but there is not enough current in my fingers, I am spent, it has taken me five hours to put together this last sentence which is insignificant and barely lukewarm; but to make note of the apocalypse I would need just half an hour of total incandescence, and this morning I am without fire, my marrow is ash, I am very sad. I had hoped to sing the death rattle, but I am voiceless. I am going to lose the apocalypse.

Tomorrow it will all be clots.

Today for the first time a present is completely beyond me. I need to wait for a bit of the past to take form so I will be able to approach this night . . .

————Already now there are ten hours between myself and madness. It is a little cooler around my eyes, slightly less fire. And then I realize that it was absolutely impossible to write in the apocalypse anyway. Because on the inside there is only the immediate present thundering past, there is only the present and a present that goes by like lightning, flash by flash, goes by spearing and striking fire, every instant cuts through and there is not even the tiniest instant of past or future in which to set one's pen or slightly sidelong thought. During the apocalypse there is only a vast pit of boiling present into which one falls. One is in the center, there is only center, no edge, no end, no door, one never stops falling, the present is black and wide, or really it is the heart itself, there is only an abyss where one dies, dies screaming . . .

Now I can start again. This apocalypse took place three days ago. The present that had been uprooted and swept away is back again after the cyclone, fresher, more transparent, and more present than ever. During the apocalypse we hurt so bad that our screams were loud enough to outrage the whole neighborhood, we actually called for death to come, and what kept us from going away with our deaths, was that each of us wanted only her own death but absolutely forbade the other death to come near. And yet, they were both there trembling with desire, my death and your death, and we felt agonizing jealousy, we shouted: "I want to leave!" "Don't go!" "I am the one who will leave!" Both of us wanted to go without going, not to stay, to tear out a life, a heart, a tongue, it didn't matter whose, I have only a faint memory of this colossal event, if neither one of us is dead it is because our deaths fought unmercifully, they threw themselves against walls, they leapt out windows, they killed each other on our bodies, they left us lying there breathless, fireless, passionless, presentless, outside of everything, outside of time, outside of paradise, outside of hell, nowhere, outside our bodies and our heads, without madness and without light, with barely a hint of memory and minimal determination to live.

I am sorry I am not up to saying more. During the apocalypse I was sure there would be no afterward, I took no notes, anyhow I would not have had what it takes.

I remember too that I was ashamed: I thought all this turbulence was hideous, it upset me to see us turned into wild animals, my claws, my chops, my fangs, disgusted me, to have come to this! that this could really happen to us! only terror from here on in, and so no more peace ever again? to have to be afraid of suddenly turning into a she-bear or lioness or hotheaded mare? To have to be afraid of oneself from now on. Afraid of biting when it is time to kiss? How fragile and delicate love is, and how powerless to resist when our ferociousness is turned loose. I was ashamed, terrified, and full of pity. And also I was totally hopeless for two days: hope too had fled and it was not coming back. I thought it would never come back ever again. During those two days I did nothing except slowly crawl back into myself; because I had gone so far that the return exhausted me, whereas Promethea returned home faster than I and took one jump through her window: she had fallen from the fourth floor (like in a play by Kleist) right beneath our window. That is why she was back in the present more and sooner that I: we had interpreted the event differently. For me it was none other than tragedy. Every characteristic of the genre was there to be seen: unity of space, time, and action, destructive emotions, the fatal irreversibility of the course of events, souls in ruin, annihilation of the Happy City, people and principles dispersed for eternity.

But Promethea's version was completely different: she never gave up imagining an uncatastrophic ending. This is impossible! I was shouting. It's all over! In my pain it was natural for me to exaggerate, because I was in such a hurry to see this night come to an end. So my shouts contained a certain amount of news that was not yet true. I don't know now if I believed it. I know Promethea didn't. Even when her death almost conquered mine and won out, she was still positive that this rage too was a form of love. I thought she was truly mad: love? this massacre?—Yes, love caused this battle, love's might and main, besides only love has the power to bring death into the midst of life, to give it orders and counterorders, to invite it in and send it away just as sincerely.

During the two days I spent in this unpleasant, too lightheaded state (my brain deserted by most of my thoughts following the bombardment) I considered Promethea as a foreign power, raving on in some other language than mine. Maybe in her country they call it love when, faced with someone deprived of her own right to die, one wants to die of rage? I watched her from quite a distance.

And then suddenly, with no warning, toward the end of the second day, hope returned. And my soul came around at the same time. I awoke next to Promethea. Life is so strong when it is given a chance to start up again! With a magical burst of hope everything went back the other way. Ever since yesterday I have been enchanted by things that made me groan in shame, and I delight in it all: both shame and enchantment. I revel in things I hated. I am happy to have been cast into the strange frozen empty abyss so full of voices where I was slowly tumbling. A priceless feeling—sadly almost faded away.

I admit: love was indeed behind all this. Love's force, love's fault. To fall so far one must be way up high to start the fall.

My one regret is that I never believed I would survive and so I dropped my notebook at the best worst moment. But do I really regret this?

Just a little. It was so horrible down in there, so black, so endless, so lonely, it was so pure, pure blackness, pure loneliness, pure despair. Just a little. Because, now things were so beautiful. If ever again we happened to lose our balance, just when sleepwalking through the same dream on the brink of hell's valley, if ever the magical mare (whom I ride through the night air hollowed out into caverns and caves where wild animals live) in a crazy fit of anger over some word I might have said without the perfect sweetness that works on her like a charm, if ever the magic Mare looks over her shoulder and whinnies: "So! You don't love me!" and bucks me off, sends me flying to the hyenas, if ever the paper ladder that I climb so easily to go pick stars for Promethea—at the very instant that I reach out my hand and it smells like fresh new moon, so good, it makes you believe in god's genius—if ever at that very instant my ladder catches fire—because it is so fragile, all it would take is someone's brushing against it tactlessly and all that would be left is ashes—if ever I had the dreadful luck again to find myself falling screaming down into the cruel guts of separation, and emptying my being of all hope, down to the last milligram of hope, until I am able to melt into the pure blackness of the abyss and be no more than night and a death rattle,

I would really rather not be tumbling around without my pencil and paper.

But this is an aesthete's thought. I have others like it, they are luxury daydreams. When one has at hand all the paper and all the time one wants, they can be permitted. I can want everything as long as I am solidly planted on the ground, in broad daylight, far from the edges of the world, high, high above any abysses, alone, with no one to hear my wishes or take the risk of granting them, except myself. I can want to write hell. But if God hears me I beseech him not to pay attention to my daydreams. Pay attention only to my fears, dear God. And then I know: no one writes hell inside hell. But what a temptation!

I think about the books I will never write, that I will never read perhaps, books that are nonetheless written, are being written in the depths, books I love, it is for them that I lean out so dangerously over the edge of the abyss. Hoping to decipher them. I am so happy they exist, I am not sad, I feel them murmuring very far away, I think about the books being written too far from eyes, and I am delighted: I have to go even farther; deeper; I know the direction life must take. I know that in the cave I did not go down into, there is a treasure and that makes me radiantly happy. This happiness is itself part of the treasure.

I saw the book of Promethea's heart. I could not read it: it was closed, held far from my face deep in a dream from some other time. But it was shown to me, I had time to see it. It exists, by god, I always suspected it and now I have seen it. It is a little book. That is something I never dreamed. Obviously the book of burning truths can only be a slim one, condensed and compact—the way all our immense passions fit into a little heart—I was blessed with seeing almost all of it. I saw its proper name and its common name. This book was called *Below* for the outside world. And for those who were close, the passionate ones, the strange tribe of those who want to know, its name was incredibly daring. A name as unique and fabulous and risky as the name of some god of words. A name composed of several different colored words. A name that spoke several languages at once.

(I wrote it down, I lost my notes in the staircase of the dream. But do me the honor of taking my word for it.) It was a magic name: just reading it I knew everything that was in the book, obviously not in detail. It is the strongest, most beautiful, the freest and most innocent book in the world. The author as a child is in it. I saw her face, from the first words uttered in the cradle, to the poem that is as great and small as a pocket star, I saw her face radiant with fearless, pitiless knowledge, I saw the Genie—a little girl who is incapable of not daring, incapable of being afraid. She wrote this book long ago, such a long time before me, it might be a hundred years or five thousand years, at any rate she wrote it at an incalculable distance from my short reach. And having written everything, yes, put everything into this unique cup, her blood, her voyages, her returns, her outbursts, her breakups, her lonely moments, her griefs, and in the end her smile, and having understood everything and seen everything there is to fight against or to love in the universe, she did not add a single word, oh, this book, this heart, this detachment, she left it there where I saw it, all the way down at the bottom of the world, and she went away somewhere else to spend the rest of her life differently, a life almost mute from now on, in happinesses and sorrows unsullied by any names.

Am I going to go down into the shaft as far as the chamber of Dreams to take the little book in my hands and climb back up to read it by our outside light?

I want to go down next to the book, I want to look at it close up, I want to stroke its dark red membrane, with my eyes closed I want to hear its song beating in the palms of my hands. I do not want to look at its warm, naked words with my reader eyes, I do not want to try and exploit its knowledge. Things written so freely are made of blood and will and living phrases that need not communicate any knowledge but that cast enough of a glow to light our separate ways.

I want to hold this lamp in front of me, I am going to find my way by the light of Promethea's heart.

Promethea, in fact, comes in bearing a tray I did not ask for. But she thought she heard me wishing for it, which is true. She sets the tray down on the edge of the shaft where I am already up to my waist. The tray is the stuff of legends and at the same time it is wonderfully real: oh, dream sandwiches, slivers of cheese so much prettier than my slips of paper, radishes sliced out of love for me and love of radishes, oh, poem for every sense, a sonnet to eat. I love you, Promethea, you whose sandwiches are as beautiful as the Songs from the Deepest Shaft and far more inspired than my sandwiches. I would gladly trade "Celebrations of Hunger" for such well-turned trays. Even one or two "Celebrations of Patience" as well. All the things you give me, Promethea, to eat, to sing out, to write out!

—I couldn't resist: for me these were moving sandwiches. Not at all ordinary sandwiches. They gave me something to choose. To taste. To regret. They defied me. I could not bear making them disappear forever. What works of art we disrespectfully gobble up!

And as for me, is it easier to write hell than sandwiches? The thing is that putting a sandwich into a text requires the art of a diamond setter. The commonest element becomes the rarest for someone who works paper.

How can one convey the depths of the secret magic of fat red radishes?

If I say, "There are some thoughtfully cleft radishes Promethea has brought me from deep inside the caves at Lascaux," will you believe me?

I still don't know if it is easier for me to measure myself against God or against radishes. But confronted with Promethea's mysteries I feel both capable and incapable of everything: I feel confident that I am able to render in writing the infinity she bathes in, but I am also sure that I am going to drown in it. Both certainties rock me vigorously on the rough water, like a seagull. I am going to fly away! I am going to dive!

What I want. Trembling with fatigue and smallness before the mountain's immensity and the magnificent depth of seas, trembling with the desire to obey my own desire (the great, abstract, and sovereign desire) I want to take the mountain into my arms, enveloping and embracing it, and feel every inch of its flanks be imprinted in my being on my skin and all the way to the bottom of my belly, I want to know the mountain this very day, this moment with no delay, I want to know it superficially, completely and internally, all the way to its guts. And faint with weakness, conscious of how outrageous this is, I want to try and decant the sea with my hands, I have decided to want things I cannot want from myself, happily and without restraint. I have decided to want to do something I have neither the strength nor the courage to do, I have decided to want to do it with all the force of my inadequacies, my fears, my little hands, my little thoughts, I have decided to try and look god in the face, as long as I could stand his rain of lightning pouring into my eyes and not die. In the hope that deep inside my eyes there will remain traces of something I would not have had the strength to see.

I have forced myself to decide to pay no attention to my own correct reasonable and obvious reasoning, and to try to do what I want to do all the while knowing that I cannot I cannot.

I want to run away, I do not want to do it, I cannot do it.

Oh my God, I must want to *want* to do what I will not succeed in doing; God make me at least strong enough to reach the foot of the mountain and break there, to wash up in pieces at the edge of the sea.

Why do I want this?

I want to be bigger, I want to climb up the paper ladder and come up to Your Highness? I want to add words to my hands so I can touch you better, I want

I want to step dripping wet from the vast adored, I want to collapse on the beach, trembling from what she made me feel as she rolled me under her velvety wave, and I, grain of sand, I want to sing her.

I want this: slowly to sink into her body, slow and breathless to go down inside her heaving breast, to let my soul sink down far from duties, from conversations, far from myself, toward her, far from me toward *"the" "source,"* far from History, far from weapons, far from sciences, toward she-who-does-not-know-she-knows-more-than-everything.

I want this: I want to tell this—feverishly transferring onto the map of the world the paths cut toward eternity.

To try to name the . . . to try to name this . . . without naming it, to try to surround this . . . so Immediate, this so real Real, this so open Flame, with thousands of drops of salt water—these are my tears of humility, these are the traces of words that I toss back into the sea—be quiet—don't touch, don't name, bathe, cool off, lick your lips, drink your tears, to try just foaming with she-who-knows-more-than-those-who-know (though she herself does not know it) nearby.

So many things I know, but I don't know how I know them, things Promethea makes me know—the way she has of making me know them without telling them to me—her wonderful way of telling a story without denouncing it, of making you understand her tale by telling the underlying tale, her way of lighting without a lamp—that is what I should so like to capture without using my sharp-toothed words, or my clawlike fingers, that is what I would like to lure pulsating into tender palms of paper. I would like to photograph the warm fresh quivering of the magic Mare's nostrils and be myself the film, the light, the caress, the fantastically silky skin of the mare's lips.

Why?

Because I now know secrets that Promethea has confided in me, ones I have never heard mentioned. I never knew that the softest skin in the whole world is the skin of a horse's nose and lips. Now I understand. I see the world in a whole new way, my sensuality is savoring a revolution. Is this a little secret? For love it is a very important secret: because if you have ever touched this ultimate softness, afterward you feel your love relaxing and extending, and you feel love spreading all over the earth, through every species, and it becomes more open and more than human and therefore more human as well. It is hard for me to explain, because I have barely started learning how to know by touch, using my hands. But this little secret about nostrils is also a key for entering the world through the door Promethea: and then you come to somewhere I had never been. And yet it is still the same world, but now it seems free of the old evil spells that make us see it as dark, silent, dirty, sad, and cynical. It is our first world, the new world, eternally new, resounding with energies and sympathies; the wondering world filling us with wonder; the world a child again and again and again; the world with a fabulous wealth of golden beauties and beauties worth a dime a dozen, a wealth of the goodnesses of comfort and of destitution; the world abounding in gazes as trusting as foals, in powerful and maternal gestures, in possible unions, friendships, silent and eternal engagements concluded in the spell of an ephemeral moment yet made of the most perfectly pure water; the world teeming with chances, large, full, patient, always there and ready to play with us.

How does it happen that ever since Promethea arrived in our city the fish have returned in vast shoals and extinct species, how is it that the sea knows something about this and how did the dolphins find out? Promethea tells me I am not objective. But for the dolphins, at any rate, my attention hasn't wandered these past few years. Or else everyone had their eyes shut.

I do not believe in magic or in parapsychology, as I have said elsewhere. But I do believe in poetry. I believe that there are creatures endowed with the power to put things together and bring them back to life: I do not know what these powers consist of but I am not alone in feeling their effects. Travel and you will see cities covered with dust, and you will see cities as shining and resonant as crystal glasses. Someone is there. This was something acknowledged in the Bible. We want to forget it, but God, or whatever replaces God, is never wrong.

But what astonishes me most, and so often astonishes me least (and I still wonder how to speak of it if I decide to try), is that Promethea loves me and I know it. More precisely, this is how it goes: "I know that Promethea loves me." It is not love that astonishes me, naturally Promethea loves, loves me, loves you, has loved. What is astonishing is that in spite of all my ordinary and extraordinary, old and well-founded resistances with regard to any such conviction, I could not deny that it has taken root inside me, with no shadows, no doubts. Anyone who knows me at all knows that this could not be easy for me or a decision I made. But Promethea's love has something in it, some chemical, or else some grace that is very active, acting gently but urgently: I know, I cannot not know, Promethea's love puts up with no uncertainty. This is not a matter of advertisement, assertion, announcements. I said "chemical" on purpose: it is almost purely internal—a blood knowledge that I feel mingling with all my substances. I am infiltrated. I am loved. It is a new feeling. I feel marinated, delicately, to the marrow. I know I smell like honey. I give off a slight fragrance: I smell it clearly when I come back in my room and suddenly find traces there of my own soul scent.

Never before had I felt so organically and so sweetly changed. I know a bit about love. I have always been a passionate devotee. But it is true that, until not long ago, in my thick-skulled naïvete, I had always contented myself with loving. I thought that was enough. A level-headed stance, daring but without any real risk: I have loved, immensely, at great cost to life, soul, and inspiration. I abandoned myself to my passion for loving with my own particular taste for inordinate splendor, and all the more freely because it all depended on me. What stunning prodigality, what fluent effusion: I had only to flow. What could be more natural? And if I was also loved, so much the better. But I never needed any assurance that there would be an exchange when I loved. I have loved people who are loving. But I have also loved gods and people I have dreamed; I loved my own father, who was gone, without burdening myself with worries about age or generation or bonds of kinship; I have loved dead women in spite of death; I have loved as I pleased, with the most authoritarian naïvete; I have engaged in love (I finally see) with splendid ardor and violent good conscience; yes, I have loved very hard without asking questions and without excuses, gallantly, unselfishly, devotedly, etc. . . . with plenty of those somewhat dubious qualities that give great souls their style. I have always loved loving a lot.

Is that called love? Now I don't know anymore. Ever since Promethea drew my attention to the other part of love, I am no longer sure what to think of myself. I find myself puzzling. Ever since Promethea asked me, "Have you really said that I love you?"—and I was surprised that I had not said it, and then I felt mortified at how extremely hard it was to get these words from myself. I was not expecting things to take such a turn. And then—this stirs up a lot of agonizing questions, new ones, old ones; also strictly philosophical questions, but I don't want to linger over those. My guess is that I could very easily be both particular and disinterested in my reflections and I would take advantage of this to spare myself any questions thrusting too close to the heart, ones that might possibly ruin the agreeable portrait of myself from which I have derived so much strength and satisfaction.

Let us be ruthless: I am loved by you, Promethea. And it is love to say that. I love you, Promethea. This is how it is, so immodest and so unmerciful, love. What a hard time I had getting up the courage to accept! Giving requires no courage, but to receive love so much strength, so much patience, and so much generosity must be extended. Only then can love descend upon us the way it wants, in one of its bewitching forms. Sometimes it opens eagle wings and swoops down on a heart to rip it out with one thrust of its beak. And sometimes it slips between our breasts like my tame squirrel. And always it makes itself felt, warm, sometimes merrily cruel, sometimes frail, and always feverish, savage. And with flesh and bone and sharp talons and with all its big or little body it weighs and weighs, it does not leave itself to the imagination.

Oh, Promethea, how I am loved by you! How you weigh upon me, how you heave me and crush me, how you besiege me and feed me, a transfusion that is marvelous but frightening, but intoxicating. So this is what that herbal potion was all about. What a drunken binge! Sometimes I would like not to drink anymore. Sometimes I am completely steeped in proud exultation.

And I? I want to take you, you who are mine, I want to take your city, which surrenders to me in vain, since my dream is to conquer it. This is what it's like, you put me in strange Christian moods, Promethea, I don't understand it at all. I want you to be the Holy City, that is something that I wanted maybe in another life; maybe a thousand or maybe five thousand years ago I besieged you; I have already contemplated your ramparts with an adoration torn between the need to protect and the desire to destroy; Oh Uruk! Oh Jerusalem! Oh Troy! Oh Carthage!

I want to take you so I can convert you to my faith, which belongs to no religion, I want to convert you to my woman's faith. That is something I did not know, you are the one who magically made me understand it, I would like to occupy you, I dream at your gates of establishing myself firmly throughout your temples, your streets, your squares, your theaters, your museums, I would like to dye your guts and your memory with my saffron, my alchemical powder, I would like to lick your viscera with my lyrical tongue, my oriental witching tongue, I would like to paint the walls of your heart and your sexual organs with my magic saliva, I would like to recreate you from within according to my plans, during your sleep, I would like you to go to sleep, You, barbarous and civilized, and then wake up singing in a language that was either Greek or mine, but I only dream of doing all this, I want to dream it, you are the one who blows on my dream fire and keeps it going, in my dreams I possess every daring and every cruelty, but in reality I would be sad if you fell, I just want to starve you a little—all the better to feed you immediately, I want to surround you, I want to court your mystery, I want to smell the fragrance of your heart, but I don't want to get anything—at least not that I know of—not right now, I want you to be strange, I want to collide with your transparencies, your crystal walls, I want you to be revealed, solid and virgin, I want only to imagine how I could achieve your transmutation, but how terrible if I tried, if I succeeded, if I lost you! As far as war is concerned I am truly a woman: I do not want to win, if I were victorious I would be the one defeated, I only want to make my desire to encircle you triumph, my desire to fly over you, to flood you, to observe you from way up high and then through a microscope, I want to know you by means of every science and every art, but I want you to keep yourself intact, you my still-brutal and imposing civilization, I want you purely Infidel if my origins are in the Faith. If I am a Jew, be an Arab and let me love you, let us love each other with our two different innocences, and if I am a woman what

I want is for you to be, to my surprise, the most profoundly unknown woman, the one most impenetrably open, the one most obviously mine, most strangely mine, that I know. I do not know you, Promethea, I still have never known you, I see that I have not yet gone into the heart of my Jerusalem, I still have you to know, I see that I shall always have you to know, my whole life I shall have you to know, my treasure. Oh, what an endless discovery it will be, from one surprise to the next, I will be struck, I will be more and more astonished, as I am already more astonished this morning at having gone so far without the center being any nearer, you open the door and once again a gaze so terribly sweet blows out of your eyes that my soul is stunned by it, I am going to fall! What a strange pain you are inflicting on me! My head is turning. I put my paper ladder up against your lovely wall, I almost reached the top, maybe I would have looked down on some view, some landscape, maybe I would have been able to take a photograph, but one look from you knocked me down, I can see this look and do not know how to describe it! Its power, its sweetness, its torrent, yes, its whirlpool, its cry, its silence, its tale, its promise, its lake of underground tears, its grace leaving the water, a nymph with hands full of pearls stretched out toward my hands.

I cannot describe this look, all the things flashing and pouring from it, its sediment, and everything it tells for all time, and its stream of silky lights, this look that bubbles up as if you had uncorked your soul's bottle and this is all the secret oil of your life that suddenly you are pouring on my face. Ah, Promethea, dear god, don't open the door while I am laboriously distilling my language into my special dish of paper, don't just open the door simply and naturally as if you wanted to bring me a cup of tea, don't open the door while I am begging the paper to turn into a winged mount that will help me chase the enchanted doe who runs faster than my arrows of thought can fly, don't open the door, don't throw this handful of pearls down before my mounting. I would need a hundred years to discover their secret, leave me, please, curled up under my paper carapace to creep slowly over three or four of your footprints; I would like, at least, to manage the simplest of notations.

This is just my luck and my great problem: I love, I want to do this lovework of mine, my paintings, my songs, my explorations, my captivating embroidery. But I am loved, the doe I am pursuing turns back toward me and all I want is to die immediately, here, on the grass or on the paper, and be born again a doe or whatever she wants to be with me.

Then I would like to moan: just stop loving me, Promethea, long enough for me to finish writing this page.

Yet I am belling with joy already.

So nowadays I work mostly at being loved. That is what worries me and frightens me the most, what makes me jump highest, and sometimes gets me somewhere.

As for what the worries of being loved are all about, I am just beginning to find out. I feel a splendid urgency to let something of this come to light in my notebooks, but am I intelligent and skilled enough, is my pride in the right place (and besides is it pride or humility that should guide me)?

And above all do I have art enough for two, will I know how to present Promethea in person in a way that does not betray her, displease her, or surprise her other than by the striking similarity between my described Promethea and the precise one that she herself, in person, would really like to be? "I would like to be the way you see me," she says, when I tell her about Promethea on certain starry nights in which I dare approach her nakedness with my completely naked voice. "So then you are the person I show you, glistening in the flow of my voice. It is really you, dripping wet, who comes out of my soul under the stars."

I know how to tell things: that is not hard, I follow the current of the river at my mare's trot and I read aloud the stars' course in the water. I only have to say what I see. But to put it down in writing requires a freedom, an assurance that I really do not possess.

This morning, for example, I am all nervous and uncertain. There is a storm, that's true. But that isn't it. Promethea is out on the water, in a sailboat, that's true. It is obvious that my thoughts inescapably turn to the author of *Prometheus Unbound,* and I feel a little seasick. But that isn't it. There is also something Promethea said at dawn when she opened her eyes and saw my face. She said: "If, one morning, you didn't love me I wouldn't try to hold onto my life, I would plunge the big knife into my heart." (The big knife is the one we just bought at the hardware store, a wonder that cuts everything from tomatoes to meat and heedless fingers, as if its blade were slicing water or air.) At these words, alas, I saw it all. I saw the knife. I saw Promethea's breast, I saw her right hand, which is a marvel of Greek sculpture. It could be the hand of Tanaïs, Penthesilea's grandmother. It is the large hand of a young woman ripe for life or death and entirely capable of cutting off her right breast if she feels that, to suddenly change History's course, she must make such a sacrifice. Ah! Already I saw the knife passing through flesh almost by its own trenchant energy, and I saw it go into Promethea's breast, I know exactly where, the precise point among all the endless constellations of her skin, I saw it go gently in, the way I always dreamed of going into the tenacious silk of her breast myself, I no longer know if I have been as far as her heart, I don't know if I have seen it, because at a certain moment my own heart released a bitter juice into my breast, the way an octopus vomits ink, I tasted the bitterness of my own blood throughout my arteries, and then I don't know what happened anymore, I found myself bending over Promethea, the way Gilgamesh, dreaming in the public square at Uruk saw himself bent over an ax as if it were a beloved woman, I saw myself all over again, I was bent over Promethea as if she were an ax ready to strike me and already I felt split open, my soul divided, I don't know if I took your heart in my hands, Promethea, that is what I must have done. But I don't remember, the vision of that moment has not stayed with me.

But that isn't it. Not these words. Not this vision. Not this black sky keeping me slightly distraught and not far from paper this morning; I hear it rustling in the shadows and I can't quite put my finger on it. Yet I'm not afraid. It is something else. Maybe it is really this piece of my paper that I found on my own table a few minutes ago, after Promethea embarked, when I had just rolled up my sleeves?

Yes, it is this sheet of paper, after all, that suddenly stopped me as it fell across my hands, an almost completely blank sheet, except that on the left side was marked diagonally, "I love you," penned in broad strokes with that strong, mad hand that is capable of anything.

Is that it? Yes. It is something big as an arbor vitae and light as a doe, something simply epic and staggering, there is a cold, stinging wind rising from these signs, I don't know how. In the legs of the letters there is an energy that carries my soul to the Tigris and then to the Ganges. I hang on, trembling like the turtle who rides through the air, carried by wild ducks, I don't dare open my mouth anymore . . .

I have put myself down . . . And now put a question to myself, the question exciting me most keenly, the one I will never get rid of: will I someday be able to write a three-word palace? Will I find the formula that makes a flourishing city appear, one full of tragedies and comedies, in one breath? Will I be able to paint the head of god, if, indeed that was what I saw, drawing the clouds that darkened the bay this morning, in just a few lines? But I don't have Promethea's potent Tuscan calligraphy. I have to make a thousand marks just to travel one of her great footprints. Just one stroke of her hand and there is an astounding picture of the famous polar day that froze all of England in February 1592. One stroke of her hand and the Thames is gleaming. The whole Renaissance is there to contemplate. But it takes me at least fifty pages packed full of words going nowhere and a very indulgent zephyr to wing me while I scribble on the glazed paper at top speed.

I love you, Promethea; but I don't have the talent to portray you alone and all at once in the one true portrait of your vast natural grandeur. And yet I see you all at once. It is my hand that is incapable. You deserve the art of Michelangelo. Mine is myopic and minutely detailed; I can only copy you very, very close up. It is scrupulous. But I sense the horizon is missing as a result; I put in all the stars, but I can't convey the sky.

What comes next is, therefore, no more than star gathering. I am charting your skin; my hands are too small to draw your grand continental dimensions.

What I am trying to do is actually way over my head. I want to make a sort of vast frieze: I am stretched out on a paper scaffolding several yards high with my face turned toward the wall of the secret cave where I have set myself up. In this position I feel closer to my model than when I am hunched down behind the ramparts of my desk.

I am a bit sad: no matter how high one is one always writes small. I would have liked (me too) so much to film Eternity! To stop one fine instant and take it close up. Filming the way we live: slow motion or speeded up, skimming over time, with all our memories brought together, with our memories of different yesteryears, with east and north, deserts and citadels, with the lightning memory of the future, with our fates foreshortened, every instant with its radiant procession of reminiscences, forebodings, impending transmutations, with all its sparkle, its shadow, its echoes, and always the heart's music that one would need a sound track for, but on paper all one can reproduce is colors—with an occasional descent into hell one gets to go through real bodily passages, anatomically and furiously, and through the heart in labor!

And what else? Everything unsayable: laughter. Our cosmic mental geography. Our joyful megalomania, our coronations, our dates with the gods. Our humors. Our waking up together between Annapurna's breasts, or one of us in India and the other just then in the Gironde, shamefully, and the next day? One in Tokyo and the other in Los Angeles because we took the wrong dream gates, but both of us just as far, far away from here, and both of us just as angry, glaring across the world red-eyed teary looks.

I am *very* sad! I am coming back to capture the moment with my turtle art, the art of a turtle mad with wonder and almost, every now and then, consoled for not being a wild duck. Under my very nose it is all so beautiful. It makes me want to sing. With words? Yes. Sometimes I think a moment is so beautiful. I want to toss it handfuls of delicious words so gluttony will keep it there.

Sometimes it makes me want to weep words, to pour all my eyes' words on her face.

(If you don't understand my contradictions I won't be hurt. I don't ask anyone to understand me. I only ask for a little patience. But I know no explanation is necessary for anyone who loves.) Sometimes (I already said this) I want to give a living moment names, as if it were an ephemeral but eternal person. Or a new star up above in our time.

What is coming now is one of these boundless, purely interior moments, a tiny fragment of depth that I am going to fish out of the river Love with my own hands, and there is nothing I can do with it other than put it, wet and twitching, onto the paper.

I have to go in
You are so naked
I have to go in. All I have left to do is go in. You are so naked. There is no door. No skin. You are so unveiled. There is no edge. Nor do I have a wall anymore, no exterior, my makeup has melted, you are so nakedly naked, so glowing, your face carved out of light instead of skin, what a light the light that comes from blood, the rose fire blood that comes from the bottom of eyes, that comes out of wells of tears, the shining burning light of the soul, that is what your face is carved from. Your lips grow, your lips sweetly rise out of the

light of the soul, your lips, flowers growing on the surface of wells of tears. I cannot not go in. But I don't go in, I don't go in, there is no door, there is no armor, there is no mask, or enclosure or mirror or image, only soul, soul, your face rests all around my eyes, my glances float, your face wet with my tears or with your tears: the pond of my thoughts. My thoughts are young, my thoughts are violent, my thirsty young foal thoughts, my thoughts of mares still heavy with milk, my thoughts want to drink your soul, my mares want to cool their flanks off in your soul.

But I don't go in, I am already hip-deep in your eyes, I am already breast-deep in your soul. You are so wide open. I cannot stay outside. There is no outside. No sands, no promise. It is a dizzying land. It is your deep body. I have never been in such a place. Your earth absolutely and violently given. All of a sudden it is honey all of a sudden it is wine blood.

You leave me no time to despair, to hope, to despair of despair. You give me only the time—lightning flash—to desire.

Never have I been so compelled to burrow so deep inside a creature. Because there are no surroundings. No helmet, no glimmering reflection, no scales, no noli me tangere, all at once it is the garden. And before the garden? Before the garden it was already the garden. The garden with all its fragrance anticipates you, anticipates itself. And before going in she is already there.

How hard it is to kiss such a naked creature without starting to fall softly into her breast. Because there is no barrier. There instantly her palate, her throat, already in the valley of her heart, already to the heart.

One's lips must go toward this mouth while bracing with all one's body against the table, against familiar furniture, in the really exterior room. One's lips must go closer while forbidding oneself to fall, don't fall. But all that does is slow the cadence.

You are so open, I am unable to remain before your eyes,

already I stand inside your lungs, I want to caress your breasts, already I feel the moisture of your womb slippery on my fingers.

I want to have time to go in. How does one go about entering something wide open? You are impenetrable because of your nakedness. Already I am in your belly, I am splashing in your blood, I roll around under your ribs between your lungs.

(And so? Invent a surface. Give it a skin. Test it with my nails. That is why I scratched you yesterday.

Make it another skin of paper. Not just one.

A wardrobe full of pages as delicate as your skin.)

I have to go out for a moment. Wait for me. Please, I would like to find a little paper basket where I can put this child to bed.

Because nothing, tragedy or comedy, has ever been as moving as the instant we have just lived. We have gone as far as death together. Then we came back to the beginning and I brought you into the world. I nursed you. Then I took you to school . . . Then . . . It was a complete life, noble and passionate, all—happiness, hardship, misunderstandings, understanding, etc.—inclusive. Nothing spared, nothing saved, all expended.

I ought to start all over, to tell this life that was complete and lasted five minutes, but I don't have the time anymore. Another life is already on its way.

What interests me is the door, this instant's door: I must find the door into the soul that leads suddenly to a secret life. One lives completely, crying and maddening to the point of silence. Moaning ashes remain.

But then one comes back.

The door loses its power. You can only go through it once. And then? Another door, for another life, has to be found . . . (So this will also be a book of doors.)

This is what is strange: when you find yourself in front of yesterday's door you are amazed: what happened there is so much more beautiful, so much stronger than I. Yesterday I was so much more beautiful than myself. Never again will I be capable of passing through this door. Never will I come back this way. Tomorrow I shall find another door, we will go through another entrance down together into eternity, never again will we have felt such vertigo, I have not experienced this yet, I only know, because each day we climb just a little higher, that the air in this life will be more intoxicating, the dizziness more topsy-turvy, tomorrow we will love each other keener, farther, deeper, profounder, the terror will be vaster, today it is impossible, but never again will we live here I know, in this light with this innocence, never again will we inhale the perfumes of tonight,

never again will I cry out to you what I cried out tonight, I no longer know what it was, my body, the one that knows stayed with yours in this morning's bedroom, I don't remember, I don't look back, the body that will catch on fire tomorrow is getting ready, soon we are going to get up

the new ignorance slowly unfolds deep in the sky, we are red, we are attentive and ignorant and deeply moved, again, anew, we know nothing,

(*Days of Separations*)

Once at the end of the day one of us said: "Maybe we ought to be apart a little? Maybe we should put some real distance between us, so a silent and invisible distance can't descend on us like fog." Because real distance does not separate.

Then spent the whole first part of a night discussing a plan of separation. Both preoccupied with an official, administrative map. Came to an agreement over setting up the tents, chose the common ground that would separate.

Came time for each of us to go to her camp. And—then—one of us, I don't know which anymore, threw her whole weight into standing up so she could take the first few steps away, and the other one I don't know which anymore cried out you're leaving? or rather, didn't cry out, a cry fell out of her heart, before she had time to think about it, because of the pain she felt in her side where their body tore apart.

Cried and cried in such pure pain that all the plans vanished, the official, administrative map disappeared into the darkness, groping after it in each other's arms advanced farther nearer deeper all the way to the dense heart of love and there morning found them inextricably entwined into one mass of foliage, slumbering in the hollow of one same damp and defenseless sleep.

She woke up. She cries: Don't go away. Don't leave me. Swear you won't . . .

Could she swear? Maybe. I don't know.

To the child she wants to swear the way a mother lies and yet does not lie: "I will always be there."

But only to the child.

Because to the woman she loves, whom she wants to make tremble she cannot say—"always."

I don't have the courage to tell you what you have the courage to tell me:

—If you don't love me anymore swear to me that you'll tell me right away.

I don't have the courage to swear. Nor the courage not to swear.

I want to reassure you. I want to make war with you, and peace.

I want you to tremble with fear tomorrow and all your life.

Give me giving. Give me your fears so I can give you calm. Give me your thirsts so I can give you my breast.

Give me your thirsts so I can drink them, suckle me with the milk of your fears. Give me time, give me strength to take my turn at fear, me first.

Sorrow: when I can give you nothing. When all I can do is let you take what you need, which is something I cannot give you. When what you need is not my blood, or my work or anything I am rich in. When what you need is yourself. Your blood and your silence.

Joy: but then I can give you this non-gift.

Giving then is bearing gracefully being someone who gives you nothing.

A love problem:

When one becomes so rich—is poverty, in the end, the true wealth?

I am becoming dangerously luxurious. My wealth: all your morning departures brimming with returns, my eyes on your heels, your shoulders, until the end of the world, until you move into infinity. Just one look a year, just one promise would have been enough, before, to provide for my soul.

An inexhaustible anthology of morning poems: but then how was it possible to sing one more poem, a completely different poem? Now all dawns are mine.

I am going to have to invent new poverty. I am going to have to invent new strength: the strength to enjoy abundance. That requires rigorous training for the soul.

I have to grow larger, stretch farther, want harder, be faster. I have to become gigantic. Exhausting!

Incomprehensible: the need to enter her flesh, the need to sink my whole self into her belly, the need to be comprehended within her breast—without her comprehending how I have managed to occupy her, the need to understand her from within, the need to start a storm in her breast, the need to demonize her, terrorize her, turn her inside out.

Incomprehensible: the way we cannot avoid becoming primitive, ruthless gods.

The need to bring her to her knees, to get down on my knees, lower, higher, I no longer know.

It is because of this greatness. I want to have beauty sit on my knees: one only desires to make those things smaller that can never be made smaller. Give up! Never give up!

Yesterday, I felt the utmost love toward her, for herself and for all that she is. For the things composing her. For everything she does with river force. For everything she does not do on purpose.

I loved her body. She does not know it. I loved the hips she hates.

I love her where she least expects me. Where she expects me I love her. But also where she does not expect me, there I suddenly love her, I attack her.

Leave so I can move toward you.
As soon as you leave, I'll start my journey toward you. I

will already be on the road; the road will (not) be long? (Only) Like a dream. I will only spend three weeks stretching out my hand to brush your lips.

I am happy that you are leaving. Because I need to see you come panting toward me from the most faraway places. Go far, go because I want you to come, I want you to come, I want to see you coming, see you coming for a long time from so far away . . .

We have to hurt ourselves more and more to find out how to do ourselves some good.

I take back everything I told you.
So I can give it back to you soon.

Promethea went into the grocery store, and she did not buy any coffee. She went into the bakery and she did not buy any bread. She went to the market. There wasn't any coriander. There were vegetables and plenty of other things. But she could not buy anything. She went to the butcher's, it was useless, she could see that the minute she stepped in: she (H) was there too, in her eyes, her eyes full of tears in her huge face, bigger than the street, and she shed such copious tears that Promethea's eyes overflowed, all she saw was her, everywhere, that is why she bought next to nothing. She never could see anything she really wanted to buy.

Finally she had to go home and look at her really.

I must escape you tomorrow, I must run and find some separation. Tomorrow I must fast. Tomorrow I must not love you all day long out of love.

—All day long?

—That shows you the fearsome scale of love.

Tomorrow I am going away to forget you, to pass away, to sleep, to dream a dream in which I meet everyone but you, to take a little boat and instantly the land is gone, to dream a foreign awakening to you.

Up there just now I loved you so fiercely, so highly beyond

me, beyond my strength that suddenly my soul was exhausted, and with one last burst I leapt over myself, over you, and I crashed down into an ice-bound night. And there, I did not love you at all anymore. I was frozen. I could no longer stir or burn.

But you, innocent and warm, you stretched yourself out the length of my absence and once again you flooded me with passion.

I am struck with admiration in the first notebook at how, almost immediately, we had to begin inventing the slightest of separations—the least little vibration, a twitch of the lips, was enough, sometimes a shadow across the eyes, yes a quiver was enough for a minute chink to appear in our magic cave. All that because we were hurtled toward each other, one on and into the other one in the other one to the other, sinking one another together, both together into such a stunning proximity, yes we were all of a sudden so magnetized that we were thrown suddenly against each other glowing in such a fierce, such a total attraction, it is impossible to be closer, it is impossible to come any nearer; and then how is one supposed to draw near and hurl oneself?

And so immediately we shivered, scarcely, enough. One bad dream and already the abyss.

Now I know things that are flint hard, things I never would have thought of; for example: how love, when it becomes infinite, reverses and turns into its opposite, and reappears as hate, fury, terror that it can no longer grow. I learned: infinity limits love. One must never stop giving it limits to devour.

If you have not lived that you cannot understand the first notebook. Because in the first notebook, which is one of springtime, of growth, of restoration, of meals, of promises, of tasting, of driving-growing-certainty, each one seems to shiver endlessly with hunger, suspicion, cold, repulsion . . .

That was love defending itself.

Do you understand? Now I am recopying the next part without touching it. I am leaving the dates.

(Date: the fifty-third day)

—Vampire! Of every drop, and every globule of my thought a vampire!

—Tell me tell me. Speak to me speak!

—I want you to suckle on my soul. I want but am afraid.

—Speak to me, speak to me!

—And if after all this I had no more blood, no more breath, no more word? I fear but want. And if after all this my tongue was drained of blood. I am afraid that you are exhausting me. Use me until I run out—I am going to find another source, I have to find it, the deepest one, inexhaustible. It is not your thirst I fear it is if the well should run dry. My spirit's wellspring. I am rich, yet your thirst is more potent than my water. So be it. Drink me. I'll invent new water. The hard moment is when I feel dryness threaten my familiar wells. Suddenly I am afraid. Not of your thirst not of my desert (there are always other oases) but of my laziness: I am going to have to get up, walk and walk, explore myself, excavate myself, down through the sands to unknown watertables. What you ask of me is not my blood it is my greatest courage.

—Speak to me, speak to me.

—I press on my breasts, I press against my heart. Sometimes words spurt out, overabound, and I too quench my thirst in my own torrent. Sometimes, I don't know why, there is nothing left at the bottom of my fountains but damp rocks and dried out phrases, sometimes I have to dig and dig, my skin is dry, my breast full of cracks, it did not rain on my heart yesterday, my heart drowses like an animal when the sun is harsh, then I dig and scratch, fingernails in agony until I hear the first sigh . . .

—Speak to me (tell me something terrible), speak to me . . .

—And what did the mountain do with its echo?

The truth is that now maybe I can no longer just feed you the milk for children. You have grown. I have to give you foods that are stronger and stronger. My flesh is what I have to serve you.

—Take me, carry me.

—The truth is you are no longer the baby on the riverbank. It wasn't long ago that I found you in the rushes but you already want me to take you on board down to the sea, you want to stand upright on my breast, you want the high seas, open and faraway places.

You want to go sailing off to death, I know.

—Do you want that too?

—No doubt I want that too? I don't want to know. If that is what I want, I don't want you to know it.

—I don't want to tell you:

I need you to live.

Now I need your body to feed my daily being. I don't want to tell you so.

Why don't I want to tell you so?

I don't want to tell you:

Now I don't know how to live without you anymore.

Why don't I want to tell you?

Because she did not want to tell her: you are asking too much of me. I don't have enough anymore. Because she did not want to say to her: give me. Did not want to ask her. Wanted to ask her without asking her.

Sin of pride: couldn't bring herself to ask.

Sin of purity: but Promethea knew how to ask with a dreadful purity.

You are purer than I. You dare show everything my lack of

courage makes me hide: your hunger, your fatigue, your fear, your need, your egoism.

The next day:
"*Vampire*": . . .

I write this phrase, the first phrase at the top of a page, I don't even write it: I moan it, and I don't even have time to finish the line when you arrive, already you are there, you lean over me all sparkling and spangling and you tell me breathlessly:—"I was drinking you from a distance, I had stabbed my gaze into your neck and drew my bow, an arrow plunges into your back and I was drinking."

—I know, I felt it, I was going to write it.

—Show me.

—I was going to . . . I can't show you yet the mark your teeth made on my neck, I can't show you yet the shape the blood spot takes on the paper—I can't, but I want to—give you something I have not even torn from myself yet, I want to give it to you, the red milk that you are making bubble up in my breasts—I don't want to give it to you but I owe it to myself to give it to you.

Because what do I have to give you except things I must tear from myself? I can only give you the blood I draw from my blood, and the flesh I cut from my breast.

Because all I can give you is what I take from myself. Whatever I have, you already have. I don't need to offer it to you.

So then, I give it to you, this scarcely formed phrase. I tear it bleeding still from its mother's womb, I give it, still throbbing with my heart's anguish, to you.

What she learned from her: the savage courage that is called purity. She called this way of being "savage courage," because, indeed, was neither cultivated nor calculated, was a wild, immediate, incautious way of plunging into torrential life with all her body, never advancing a diffident body or a shielded soul, but offering herself unguardedly unconditionally to life's blows. If life shot one of those sudden rays it fires, one we fearful ones flee, trembling and keeping low, she would not run away, would let the arrow of light go right through her. And would sigh.

Did not flee. Did not keep low. And sometimes was knocked down by the blow. Exactly what I am so afraid of. Because real life knocks people down. Stiff and straight, I try to resist it. How? By pretending not to have felt anything.

Whereas she never pretended: welcomed everything, joy, pain, anguish. And said thank you.

(The sixtieth day already)

I know how to kill Promethea. All you have to do to kill her is tell her one of the poison phrases she entrusted to me. She can also be killed with a particular look. There is also a particular tone of voice that is very bad for her soul. She taught me all that. I know where the secret doors to her soul are. And I have seen signs of vulnerability on her body.

I did not ask her for any of this, she is the one who turned over the keys of her life to me.

I shouldn't have taken them? I wouldn't have been able to refuse them, I would have been afraid of killing her. Doesn't that prove that I already had her keys before she ever gave them to me? I don't know, I didn't know I did, maybe I took them absentmindedly? I wanted to hide them very carefully to protect her from people who might hurt her.

Sometimes Promethea's soul has just turned five. And the world around her is so fresh and new and merciless the way it always is when the world is rebeginning. Then she asks, "Would you be sad if I died?" And her eyes are both bold and submissive to reality, her eyes look straight at the strange faces of grownups who know less and less about mortality with each step they take toward death.

"If I died would you miss me?"

If one is a grownup one can choose to answer with that honest, impervious wisdom one uses to cover one's soul:

"Everyone who dies is missed by all of humanity. So you, especially, etc."

Or one can not answer.

One can answer, "Yes."

One is careful not to answer, "And what if *I* died?" Because one knows the answer. That is one of the things that would kill Promethea.

Promethea is mortal, she knows she is, passionately, the way all children know it. She gives me her life to take care of, to give her. I give it to her: that instant she is born. Nothing is more astounding than these births in the prime of life.

And what if I forgot the child? If, just once, I forgot to give her a life? That's not possible. A mother doesn't forget. But I am not a mother. That isn't possible? I am a woman. I am born a mother like all daughters. And Promethea? She too is a woman, a child, a mother.

She gives me her life and also her death to take care of, to give her. And I? I'm the one who had enough of being mortal. I was hoping never to be so again. I had said: "Get out of here death!" And ever since I had everyone believing, myself included, that dying was something I had nothing to do with. Even dying, I would not have admitted it.

What made me change? Cry?

I don't exactly know.

Maybe it was this gaze that is so transparent: I was going downstairs, I had spent two or three hours in a brief, conscientious absence in my study. At the bottom of the stairs Promethea's gaze opened up before my feet like the depths of life. Waited for me.

As I was coming down, she opened her mouth: "I missed

you," she opened the doors of her soul, I was coming down from my banality, step by step, I saw the dark and shining entrance to her soul deep in her eyes, there in those depths the wild forest begins, I went far, far down through her life, through the forest, down those stairs, to her death.

Maybe it was that slightly bitter cup of tea: maybe it was a cup of tears.

Maybe it was one of her smiles, the blessed child in the inferno who hears god singing.

But maybe it was that strange moment when I took her in my arms after an extremely hard hour-long separation, when my heart suddenly fell into her breast, my flesh merging with hers until my heart comes straight back to me. I don't know how, Promethea is part of me. What happens in her often happens in me. Sometimes I think I am suffering when she is the one who suffers writhing in my breast. Sometimes she sparkles with joy, I am glad, and she tells me that my joy makes her shine.

—Can I make you tremble?

I would really have liked to say no.

But I feel her trembling throughout my body.

—You know everything, tell me why I want to make you turn pale.

—I won't answer.

—Tell me then where you have to be hit to make the tears come? Could I make you cry?

I will not say: that is because I am a city that does not want to surrender. Besiege me. It is because I am a deep, cool pyramid. Go through me. Pass through all my rooms and know my subterfuge. But you are passing right by the little room that I want to keep closed, and you don't see it. There is a secret. I myself do not know it, I just know it exists.

All the things Promethea gave her this week, so much that she doesn't even know, nor does she herself. She is inundated.

126

She gave her: lessons of absolute humility: pure, not humble.

Tuesday's dawn she murmured: "You'll never leave me?"

An utter confidence spoke that sentence: May you have your desire, may your whim be fulfilled, may your incomprehensible will be done.

She came in Wednesday evening, out of breath; when she was opening the door she dropped everything, her bag and the big sack of books, and she threw herself down on her knees, and she clasped her knees.

And it was Thursday morning that she gave her a shot of mortality without meaning to, on the meadow filled with flowers in the middle of the garden.

This Thursday . . .

—(I'm stepping in for a second, because the end of the first notebook is coming up soon.) There was a fight between us then that went unchecked, unremembered by the notebook:

—I say "between us" but really more between two conceptions of love, of life, two versions of the essential mysteries, two ways of thinking about the presence of creatures on this earth, two philosophies, when all is said, two ways of assessing goodness, justice, law, freedom . . .

I say "fight" because we held two different positions about practically every means, but we were in agreement about the ends. But rather than fight I should say: pleading, prayer, entreaty, conversion, body wrestling. And neither one wanted to win.

Each one desired the other's victory which she opposed her with all her sincere and tortured conviction. "Defeat me!" she begged.

Both shouted "I won!" Yes, in the end there was only winning. Each of them was already a little bit the other: you couldn't really tell who had just lost a chunk of territory, who had just taken it.

The most important argument was unspoken: it was

about death. Because Promethea talks about it a lot, carelessly, shamelessly, familiarly. Bravely. But I, for a long time, I hadn't given it a thought. I no longer know when I decided not to involve myself with it personally, except as a strictly private matter: "someday I'll die," it was nobody's business, it would be an accident, without importance; I lived right, nonetheless, all I did was live and not risk losing my life, but not risk saving it either.

My state, during the period of the first notebook, was still that of someone for whom dying is precluded. For a long time I had no longer wanted to die at all. I was anchored in a pleasant bay in the temperate zone. Nothing happened.

And now?

Promethea gave me back my taste for fire.

I said yes to storms. Twice a day at least we gallop foaming with fear back into the cave while death rumbles overhead, and each time one of us is tempted to leap outside herself into its abyss. We are panicky, always alert. Never will I dare mention in these notebooks the extent to which we are teetering along the ridge of the world, for fear that I will hear myself say some of the terrible things I am trying to curb.

All that because I gave in to Promethea anyhow. I acknowledged death. Yes, we can die.

What a life ever since that day! It is such a cyclone that sometimes one could lose one's balance from the mere exhilaration and fall from life's heights. What fear! What relief! . . . Back to the notebook . . .

This Thursday:

The same garden.

I lift my head. She is gone. It is ten minutes to ten. Nothing is left but the sun. It is the sun of tragedy. In the empty meadow—thousands of hideously immobile daisies hideously white, thousands of God's teeth. Tear me apart, it's all right with me. But God too has abandoned me. And the silent meadow. The deafening sun. And no light at all. I stand up. I stay up. Maybe I am dead. Sometimes one dies. Afterward it turns out one is standing there, stunned. No one to say whether today is the dream or if yesterday was. Did I invent us then? That is the reason for holding still. I thought you were real, in my dream. Somebody one scarcely dares think about, if it is a dream, will come, will not come, if it is not a dream, will come, if it is yesterday, if someone comes, if she comes, if you come, then whether this or yesterday is the dream, it doesn't matter, it doesn't matter . . .

There she is. It is ten o'clock.

Am I still slightly dead? I look at her slowly, I am looking at her from my death. Nothing comes out of my mouth.

How I would like to be reincarnated now!

All I have left is eyes, not even that; just the edges of my eyes, the rims of gazing.

Now, with the vision granted me I recall a body, right here, in the meadow. It takes a long time. It takes pity and indulgence.

When you went away, you left me nothing but the sunbleached world. You did not even leave me a heart to bleed with. I found I was standing there with no body, and so no voice for calling you.

Wait for me now.

Now I see you, I see it all, it all comes to me, you hit me all at once, ten times I am struck by your hair, your body emits thousands of rays at me.

I am bombarded by happiness, I am pierced by life.

I come back to myself.

It begins. First the blank pain. First the fear of death. It has begun. I am already afraid. No desire yet. No. I am still too faint, too dim. I do not have enough strength yet to start dying again.

Like vomiting one's soul to present her with the gift of one's agony, said to her: be happy that you have already hurt me so horribly, be glad you have chilled me to the bone, you have turned my heart to stone, you have made my marrow into ashes, you can be glad, more than once you have made me turn pale and gnash my teeth. (Yet why did I bite my lips until they bled not to tell you this?) (because I didn't want to give you the pleasure of feeling you had the power of death over my heart) (because I did not want to deprive you of the happiness of being able to press all your weight against my heart as if it were god-the-mother's heart of steel) (because I wanted to deprive you of the happiness of knowing that you could wound me and get drunk on my blood).

And why at that moment suddenly told her everything she had not told her, and that she had sworn never, never to reveal to her? To give her two of everything: what she had hidden from her, and also that she had hidden it, and also what she had sworn, to give her everything in triplicate, a hundredfold, to triumph over herself and give her the joy of a triple victory, a triple defeat.

—Defeat me. Pillage me. If there is a house, a room, a safe in my city that I have not turned over to you, whose keys I haven't provided, if you find one single door I might have forgotten inadvertently deep inside my soul, smash it open.

What had she hidden from her? The places where death could get into her.

So she began then to undress her soul and showed her, here, almost fainting with terror, here and here, if you stab with a very sharp word you will plunge your blade all the way to the root of my life without encountering any resistance.

Secret rooms, highly protected, in which she kept life-threatening passions locked up.

Opened up the pyramid. Showed her the worst: her every ugliness, every greed, every monster, every ferocity.

With despair with joy. Gave her the portrait hidden behind the portrait of her soul in full dress. A portrait she had never told anyone about, that no one had ever seen, not even herself.

Because the height of love now was not to give just her

own beauty, but to go so far as to make a gift of her own petti-ness.

Dismantled her citadel of all her own forces.

Was stripping. Took off her plumed helmet.

Was even smaller.

If you strike now you will get me and you will know it. She had to say, "I am possessive." And she was amazed to find this out herself. Discovered the ordinary marvelous banal human violence of her emotions. So she too was a weak devoured de-vourable devouring human being?

Was discovering with terrified joy that she was capable of everything she had never been brave enough to be capable of before: for example, an ancient jealousy.

—Would I be capable of flying into a rage someday? Of wanting a dagger in my breast or in yours?

She tried to think new thoughts and guessed the answer when she felt the pain piercing beneath her right breast.

Our bodies, a mine, this history, a mine, this passion, a mine. New drilling everyday.

I close my eyes and go down into my depths, where a great whale hunt is going on. Each one takes her turn with the har-poon, and the whale.

No need.

I have what I need. Land of my own, vast for exploring, working, surveying, leaving, a land with sea along its haunches. I have what I need to live, I am at peace. I have what I need to feed my ambitions, my dreams, my extrava-gances, I have enough fire for all my passions.

All my energy is employed in the great maneuvers of my desires. That is where everything happens.

Sometimes I do not desire you.

Sometimes I desire you the way God desires his creature: I want to be your maker, I don't want you to make me. To touch you and you not touch me. Like the pleasure God takes in warming himself with his creature. While the creature shivers with cold.

Sometimes I desire you the way a queen desires a slave: I would like to belong to you and have you order me and humble me and provide me with the realm of obedience. Sometimes I want to rule over you with all the fierceness of the slave bent over the queen.

Sometimes I want my desire to torment you, and goad you and make you race around the earth in vain, billowing and crazy, until you fall down foaming.

Sometimes I desire your desire . . . sometimes I'm not hungry. Famish me.

No peace and quiet. We want storms. Nothing but storms.

Yesterday she left. What sadness! What happiness! Where? To China. Next door. To the other end of the world. She went away utterly. She was not in the house anymore. She phoned from faraway. She was somewhere over there: Far. She said: "I hurt." Thank goodness. I said: "That's good. Burn. Please burn. Otherwise I'd die of cold."

She took her presence with her. In exchange she left me waiting. Luckily I did indeed wait. Luckily she gave me her hurting to warm me up again.

Once she went away merrily, not on purpose. The whole day I lost her, I killed her, she killed me, I disowned her, the waiting was tortured, I vomited blood, I didn't tell her, I kept it a secret so I could drive her mad someday when I needed to. And then I tried to find her so I could stop this massacre. I wanted to take the first boat to go find her, to stop her being lost, to stop her forgetting me, to stop our suffering, to end the punishment, when I came to the docks, hell! I wasn't able to get her back, she was already there, she had just come back, smiling, she took her return away from me as merrily as she inflicted her going upon me. All I ever had was hurt and grief.

That was a bad day. I treasure it. I hold onto it just the way it was given to me, gray, shivering, its face grimacing in dreadful grief, its cheeks dirty with tears. I am keeping that day, it is something rare, a day insane with anger and injustice. I feel such pure meanness will not often be my luck. Sometimes I think about her (that day), I admire her viciousness, I caress her and feel once again how sharp her teeth are.

Yesterday she was sad leaving. So her return began immediately. She is coming back straight away. Every step away brings her back. That's so nice . . .

. . . everything is happy now. I am a little sad not to have time to spend all morning stretched out against your body, when the hours of the day are fast as minutes, and then to spend the afternoon immersed in your thighs when minutes are fat as hours, I am a little sad about that and I am happy about that. Everything makes us happy sad.

She came back.

I had imagined it all so perfectly, I had imagined your first glance, I had seen the fire of your smile turned toward me like a gaze hurtling out of eternity, I had imagined your body, precisely, from the blaze of your hair down to your shoes, I had imagined your color, your exact size, the way you walk.

So I was sure that nothing I had imagined would come true. But it was all just the way I had imagined. It really was you. It was really my dream, and yet it really was reality.

I am exhausted: Someone is granting my wishes to the point of exhaustion. All the things I don't let myself believe in but only dream: It is all coming true.

Someone of whom I ask nothing is giving me everything!

My God! So I am going to surrender to your strangeness, I am really going to end up believing that, You exist, as for me,

I don't know what else I can think up to give You the chance to prove You exist.

Were you written? I write you the way you were written.

You are the way I ordered you from God, exactly.

You are the response. As if I had written a very detailed letter to god. Certain I was writing to no one. So I could ask freely for everything I wanted.

And here he has sent me the Answer!

You put your mark on me: because I don't run away from you. You leave traces in me. You write me. You crowd me. You populate me. I recognized you: you are one of my people. You are my people. I don't comprehend you. I contain you. No longer am I anything more than all your sensing space.

Hard to write because of happiness. Happiness always impossible, if it is real: always blazing, unbearable.

A dream: writing fire in the fire.

Two dangers: following the other open-eyed, or eyes closed. Not easy to shut one's eyes. Or open them. Those are the two worst dangers.

I take it all: I want what I don't want too. I also want to do what I'd better not do.

Haggadah

She asks: To snatch me from death would you go a great great distance? As far as Finland?

And the answer: Didn't I take the express to Roissy?

Didn't I exceed myself going after you through all hell's stations to the depths of hell, to find you and bring you back, holding your hand and dragging you to the light, looking at you and smiling?

The answer: Finland is no farther for me than the other end of town. I went to get you at Roissy where I never would have gone. So why not go to the end of the earth? There is no difference. For me there isn't a difference anymore. Distances don't count.

That is why I was shaking all the way to Roissy. I shook. I didn't want to tell you: I'll be there, I am going to get you. I didn't want to tell you: I cannot not go and wait for you on the other side of the world. I cannot not go looking for you in Finland. I cannot not go back around the world after you.

But the thing is you don't know how frigid and faraway Roissy is for someone whose only travels have been in vast imaginary distances.

How would you know?

All the strange things, all the features I erase from my secret face, and all the pickets of the fence around my heart that I pull out one by one, the blood spurting with each pull because they are alive.

All the things I have never done, that I didn't want to do for anybody in the world, that I don't want to do, every little gigantic humble gesture, I do them for you, and they are my greatest exploits.

(If I tell you: "I'll organize your bills, as attentively as Thetis supervising the manufacture of Achilles' weapons"—it means: "I love you like the child of my womb, my only daughter, I will devise milk to nourish you even if I am ninety years old.")

A list of seemingly insignificant gestures, whose real meaning, however, is: "I am coming toward you bringing my lands, the keys to my secret safes, the combination to my soul":

—I shall go: to the movies with you. Even comedies, I'll go.

—I shall go: to a city full of unpleasant memories, one I would not even have sworn never to set foot in again, because that was so obvious. I'll go. Disgusted, fearful, apprehensive. Confidently, nimbly, elegantly, and sure of change.

—Even sew the buttons on your shirt (though it is Begonia who sews my own buttons back on).

—If you want three cats, even females, or even that many hens, fine.

—Some things can turn magical, such as: going to the Mammouth; but not everything transmutes so easily.

Particularly I have a hard time with the human beings

when you can't get away from how many they are. The same for bad little girls and their unconsciously racist mothers, I won't give in to the pleasures of scorn. As much as possible.

All the questions she never would have asked:

—If you had to sacrifice your eyes to save my life would you?

Answer: Yes.

You would give your eyes! You would give up beautiful light for me?

H's feelings: undeniable terror, pain and cowardice in advance, tears bubbling in her eyes, a violent sensation of rebellious egoism—but between the two evils, when all is said and done, there is no doubt, one is really worse than the other. H answers aghast: Yes. With delight. In despair.

Needs her eyes not just to see the world and the face of Promethea herself, but to construct her visionary world built from words on paper. Without eyes the person she is would not exist . . . Will have to learn Braille. Hurts her fingers to think of it. Makes them sad too: her fingers have never *touched* words, don't want to touch words, fingers made only for caressing, reserved fingers, fingers made for warm skin, for the supple sweetness of flesh.

—Why didn't you ask me for my legs instead? No! No! not my legs that are made to slide between your legs. No! take my eyes! Maybe you won't see that I don't see you?

Remarks:

Rereading this book I notice that it has a unity: a book on relinquishment, dispossession and possession.

It is a hemorrhage. Will stop when no more drops of blood.

Also: it takes place in the guts.

During all this time things are happening on the surface of the earth as if there were no guts.

There's nothing about Promethea's job.

There's nothing about my job either.

That proves one can have an underlife existence and that one can die or rediscover the cave paintings at Lascaux at the same time one prepares for . . . examinations, etc., universities, shows, etc.

Now I move on to the second notebook. It begins quite by accident that is maybe not all that accidental, with a long reflection on happiness as a threat to and threatened by sleep, as threatening in its peace. Those pages are paradoxical and rather cruel. I'm skipping the beginning. Then I pick up on the first day of summer.

Slightly lost, because this week happiness was so calm and innocent and so unthreatened. Never again such a peace. Which began in its peaceful way to hurt her slightly, frighten her slightly. Because one must have such an energetic nobility of soul to move forward beneath such happiness and not suddenly feel utterly powerless (thought that clumsily because never thought so high before)—powerless—enough to go even higher.

A sense of heights. And then?

A sense of being "good," that the world smiled upon her, a sense of being one of the blessed now. Was slightly afraid, of fate's goodness and her own goodness. "What trouble would she have to go to, to be worthy of such a magnificent and generous reward?" No, that isn't it . . .

But rather: "What does one do to succeed in having (anew) something one already has?"

Became acquainted with "happiness" (began to think this and shuddered—from timidity—from anxiety).

"Happiness"? What she was encountering: a kind of peace that surrounded her in every direction.

She had some funny feelings, hard to pin down, blurry like the shadows coming from the sun she bowed to and dreaded, bowed while she felt rumbling in her heart's distance a vague desire for storms, absurd, she who adores the sun.

Feelings that sent shivers up and down her and vanished before she had time to recognize them. But one of them came back several times, quivering around her heart, giving her a slight, pleasant desire to vomit until, in amazement, she had to admit it.

Felt she was a bit of a "liar." Yes, slightly fraudulent, like someone who had gotten something she had not even asked for. Or maybe not even wanted?

Deep down perhaps what she wanted was air, not earth, turmoil, fury, fire—she wanted "to lose."

To lose? Wasn't she losing?

Oh yes indeed! Lost every day the very day she was engaged in living for the first and last time.

She was engaged in losing this new childhood that had been granted her, which went by so fast it hurt. Would this summer already be adulthood?

And bit by bit she was losing obstacles. The whole world was giving way before the pressure of her desire, caving in, letting itself be penetrated, opening up sweetly moist beneath her caressing, pressing fingers, the world was not refusing her its sweet, moist depths, and she, joyfully, painfully went ahead, entered, sensed the promised bliss that was on its way, that was going to come, that would not be long in coming, not waiting—and bit by bit she was losing the distance, the delay, she was losing uncertainty.

My god, don't give in too fast, she begged.

Threaten me, resist me. But at the same time she was caressing her with a more and more exquisite and urgent and suppliant precision, she begged her: oh give me, come, give in to me, she wanted to win and in her effort to conquer she was giving her all.

(I no longer know if "she" is Promethea or me, in these notes.)

But Promethea was the first one to say "the terrible things" in the next pages. Because she is innocent enough to be able to play with death, like the little boy with the satiny coals: poetically and religiously. What "terrible things"?

She dares say. Really terrible things. That I would never dare say. Why? Dumbfounded. I know things. But I cannot. Would I like to? I think so.

Fear of making her suffer? Yes; fear then of making myself

suffer. One can imagine her being tortured. But how hard to picture oneself as the torturer.

—Try!

I try.

—Hit me! Give it to me! I want to give you my blood.

Tries and tries unsuccessfully to raise the knife, only raising a strange invasion of shame.

Stretched out on the great white doe, feverishly seeking the words that would finally slice into her flesh.

None come, none come.

And her, spread out, it was as if Promethea was waiting for her eagle. But the eagle doesn't come, doesn't come; and the doe, her, feeling so hungry, so hungry for that pain.

Then finally, the eagle came, but it was such a tortured, clumsy eagle, one weakened by love. Then what? Tries with all its body to do its duty. Extended its neck, struck—but the blow trails off in the slowness of dream.

Until, in the end, obviously the cruelty was not dealing the desired blow, dealing instead twenty blows that are disappointing and offensive to the greatness of the creature who wanted to make an offering of sizable suffering. Finally.

Then, hesitating no longer, not searching, not thinking, not planning, took a dreadfully rusty phrase, not even one of her own, and thrust it into the beloved flank so passionately that, losing her balance, she herself suddenly hurtled into the abyss—and she rolls and rolls like a little bloody pebble all the way down the mountain; and lies where she landed, unable to get up. The grass is green, her tears are so salty. Her limbs no longer obey her will.

She can neither raise nor lower the mountain.

(Egoism: rather than obey you, I hurt myself; I wanted to make you taste death and kill myself instead.)

—Tell me, you who can read, what explains this need to lean so calmly so far out the window that the fall will be only up to fate?

Promethea clasps her in her arms (as if her name were Perdita) as if she wanted to embed her in her heart so she would never again be in danger of getting lost.

When all the caresses one wants to lavish turn into the thrusts of talons, when one faints with sweet pleasure at the thought of slowly tearing apart a breast, is that love?

In the second notebook up and down are frequently turned upside down, things are frequently reversed: one into the other, one sort into another, fire into ice, blood into stone, and stone into tears. This notebook is very restless. With a single page it races across big countries, through Quanzhou, through Scythia (where Promethea comes from), it crosses the Caucasus Mountains and the Himalayas, and lands occasionally in some inn in Constantinople. On the next page it is on the banks of the Seine, in the meadow embellished by an old and strangely familiar dwelling; but is there, maybe, only one river that transforms itself as it goes around the world?

This notebook is our hippogriff: we never know where it will land because it takes off so suddenly. One page it's India, one page it's Vienna, one page it's home, one page it's the desert. We don't decide the time or place.

With a look from one of us the forest catches on fire, the hippogriff flies off again, one of us stays behind, one of us thinks she will die, one becomes Olympia, she turns into stone on the suddenly deserted page. It is the end of the world for an hour; and then the hippogriff comes back . . . etc.

This notebook is full of fantastic incidents, both fascinating and painful.

Naturally the only order it has is geographical.

Desires work wonders. As if two magics had fallen in love with one another.

H's desire: to overturn the mountain, to caress her until she turns into a foaming mare, and then, leaping onto her, to grip her warm flanks with bronze thighs, to spur her with bronze spurs, to lacerate her haunches, to make her flanks and belly bleed,

until she turns into a lionessdoe

until she turns into a fawness

to rock her, to take her in her lap, suckle her, until she falls asleep full,

to breathe a magnificent dream into her, through the mouth, through the ears

until she wakes up a mountain with icy torrents cascading from her neck all down her chest

Desire to knock her down and pick her up, to tame her and let her run away, in spite of myself.

She does not resist. Stretched out, voluminous, she does not even surrender. She has already surrendered. Impossible to make war on her.

And I, then, finally, defeated, all that is left for me is to submit to reality. Fine. I will not provoke you. I will not kill you. Alas. I will not fall on you and beat you hard with my black wings. Defeated, defeathered, bare-armed, all silk, I am going to cradle you, I accept being separated from you, once again, to separate you from me, to give you a birth. I am going to return anew to life's entrance. For you, the new first step.

For you, I am turning myself into a mother painfully and passionately, since that is what you want, I am coming apart.

And now, be born.

12/6

So many feelings I never felt before. For example? I never felt, for example, this needle keen burst of anger that stabbed me in the breast sometime after you told me they had vaccinated you. Because at first—nothing happened. But suddenly two hours later, as if the needle that touched you had taken all that time to become real for me, the idea of that touch, the idea of . . . that look . . . inevitable, on your skin—the idea of those eyes—the idea, on your flesh; on your skin, the idea on your nakedness—the idea behind the look—on your backside, looked at, on your flesh, the look, the idea, suddenly turned around, the needle, stuck straight into my breast, here, but not enough, not far enough, the idea hurt me just hurt me, made me mad—I tear it from my breast, there is someone I want to stab, there is someone I would like to make vanish from the face of the earth, there is someone who stabs me in the heart, there is someone I would like to hit, as I groan, I am at the door to my life, I am at the breast of my life, I am beating with my fists and crying. In! I want to come in! I no longer know who is entering who is penetrating who is invaded, my sense of things is torn in shreds.

I cannot say all this, I cannot escape all this, I cannot, I don't want to put out the fire, I don't want to fear the pain, all this for a needle? all this for a little something sharp that sticks into me in your flesh straight through my body and pins my soul to the door.

And then?

One can die of love. And sometimes, for love, one dies of a shot, a syringe.

I don't want them to touch you. I hate Them.

Am I ashamed? Not at all. A little.

What I am feeling: a gloating hatred for Them. I dance around Them in hate. I already danced in hate around a stake when I was three and a Sioux with a thirst for vengeance. But I became more civilized afterward, I became white and polite with clean fingernails and a level voice, and my blood especially, obedient and regular blood. I don't blush, my cheeks are virginal. But now? I know what hate is now. Maybe it's love. It is the sense of joy feeling oneself die of anger and pain for the idea of a needle's sacrilege. Everything is an arrow, everything is poison. Everything is religion. It is the sense of joy feeling oneself capable of life and death. "I am going to kill

you," I thought. It's a delicious thought. Life thought because death thought. Anyone who can give death can give
life.

I am turning into God now because of a shot; and that is
love. I have gone dark again.

Tuesday's transfiguration: this shining, lit-up world, emit-
ting luminous vibrations, magicked.

Everything in this Arabian Nights market has a charm that
is epic, a song of vegetables and fruits, strawberries cooing,
animism everywhere. Even the eggplants? Yes. Even the po-
tatoes are breathing. Even.

Promethea is buying ten little goats? Transparent goats
leap through the air.

Promethea and H have crossed the great city, it was Constantinople.

Along the way experienced every climate. Wanted to die
any number of times. Sometimes from exhaustion. Sometimes plunging into the depths of despair, knowing that it
was perhaps a misunderstanding. But the air was unbreath-
able so often. They crossed every circle of love, their two
horses sometimes winged, sometimes turning suddenly into
a car, a deux-chevaux; or sometimes a gondola. Once into a
real camel.

Coming back from the magicked market
All of a sudden one of them felt volcanic pangs of jealousy.
Unjustified, unexplainable—pure. The cup of hemlock.

The need to punish, to draw blood, this need, not being
able to satisfy it.

Eyes silently formulating what the teeth would absolutely
not let out. Gazes gripping in slow anger, silently cried out to
each other: love eats me up, tigers devour me, there is no end
to this suffering, willingly I would die, already I am dying, silently, entangled gazes moaning: put an end to me, take me
into your fire and consume me. Promethea and H are back in

front of the door, running on flames. Did they get there by land or by air? They'll never know, running on angry tears, neither of them saw, neither of them was able to tear her eyes from the eyes that held her.

When, still alive, they opened the door, it was already night.

But on Wednesday:

All of a sudden Promethea turns into an eagle. Swoops down in darkness on H. Is already turning into a lioness of the air, already needing to bite. Needs a rock, needs to attach, needs to peck, needs to tear.

They are astounded by the urgent necessity to create this scene.

—I have to strike.

—I have to pounce.

Never such a light, wheeling, assailing female eaglet. Rather than striking turns into an Egyptian boat and flies off on the wind again. And this is how, from dream to shore, they come to a heavenly India, They discover it by accident in some heaven.

Because they never suspected its existence.

There, musics, fountains, fruits, antique smiles.

Then one of them said with difficulty:

—Never, never have I felt such great pleasure

Teary-eyed. Because she had already said this.

—You already told me that.

—Yes. It was true.

I didn't know. I didn't know there is a heaven after heaven.

And since she had never felt such trust, truly, a trust based on trust, she left it absolutely up to love. All the way up to its unbounded enjoyment. Now she wanted to die and could not die. Called on God. Help. Wanted to die because could not die. Could no longer stop living, enjoying. Wanted to die to start all over again. To stop enjoying. Because the enjoyment exhausted her, killed her, ejected her, threw her out of the world, into burning sweet chaos, where she wandered lost and exorbitant, out of orbit, out of her own womb, out of her sockets, disconnected uncentered rays, all her flesh scattered like stars, bones light as feathers. And if the sea herself were not there to fish her back, to pick her up, to make her all over again, never would she have found face again. The sea? Yes, the sea, with her great deep blue hands and her silver mane, whinnying as she gallops west, or east of the volcano, where she was still erupting, spewing litters of sparks, bellowing incandescence.

—I am being killed by what keeps me from dying.

And next the sea became very small no bigger than a bathtub. Rolling in pain crashed over and over again onto the edges of the world. Then a divinity fished her out. The Deity held her by her gills, by her genitals.

What fantastic sensual pleasure is inflicted by the Deity, holy and terrible.

And how to drown? how to get away?

—As if the sea herself were holding me, the sea throbs in my belly, the sea licks up into my loins.

And then, with a start, taking the astounding passage, through the straits separating the continent of me from the continent of you, we reach infinity: there, it is as if there were only one desire, one divine power, one thunderbolt, that God granted now to one, now to the other.

And suddenly Promethea is the one struck and galvanized by it. The previous moment brought down, the next moment standing, gigantic, ready for triumph.

In the car at night, Constantinople, Saturday.

Never stops looking back, the magic mare, twisting her great bird's neck to see if you are there, if you are there, you are there, because I don't feel your weight on my back.

Straddle me, dig your spurs into my sides, I am so afraid that I am dreaming that I carry you off, you my love my mistress, carry you off into my starry lands, I am so afraid that I am dreaming, reality is so strangely fast and flimsy and transparent, the world is opening up like a curtain before my desires, everything obeys me, space floats where I want it, I am carried, I carry, hurt me, make me feel that I am not going to wake up, reality is so dazzling and so dreamy, there is no wall, no bar, no obstacle, no armies are separating us, we are not shaken by hatred.

what would be able to separate us?

I am afraid to go toward you to my farthest limits never meeting any resistance, to the end, to the edge of self, to fall, fall into you, into your delicious cool pit, to fall eternally into you, out of me, and deep within to forget me and forget me, and then with me forgotten, who, deep inside you will remember you? Who will unearth you?

What would be able to hold me back?

In the dark she said:

—"Do you know what it would be like for me if you stopped loving me?"

Why did she say it?

—"I would die if I hurt you."

"My life in your hands."

She answered: "I don't know." (It wasn't true. Guessed. But she wanted to draw a bit of blood.)

Promethea turned on her, her eyes clouded with surprise. They very nearly fell into the abyss. To avoid the chasm the mare threw herself against the steep barrier. They drove on crying.

Promethea gasping for breath, her eyes staggered by the unbearable sight as if she had seen God herself flash an ironic glance her way.

She gives me the fierce inordinate joy of ordering, the joy of giving an order, and that this order be a gift, divine joy, Promethea gives me this.

Divine, I say? Yes. Because what Promethea has made me see is how happy God must have been to be able to give orders, and his orders were gifts, given him by the world because of its love for him. Because you cannot give orders joyfully unless some very great person gives you the joy of being able to give them.

God said let there be light. And light smiled because it could satisfy God's desire. And there is light.

And I? I open the window, and the world is there on the outside, waiting to be. And in the middle of the world, deep within, and seen from above, very way up where I am at the window, tiny and dazzling like a lionessdoe painted in the heart of an Indian jungle, is Promethea, and she is waiting. Then, with an imperious and superhuman will, with a dangerous audacity, I shout an order out the window: "Come!" I shout just one word. Only one. Short. Clear. Absolute. Why dangerous? Because this word has something in it: I put my heart into this word. I slipped my heart into this little word. And I threw it out the window. Like this: Come!

That is the reason I said Come! so impetuously, in such a superhuman voice. I said "come," plain and simple, nothing else, as if I were a tyrant, I threw my order out the window, but really, yes, I put my heart into it, I put my heart there for Promethea, my own heart hurled from the upstairs window, like an order, like a gift, there it goes, dropping like a stone toward the ground, falling straight toward the center of the earth where, at the bottom, Promethea stands, it falls like a rock, like a meteor, falls, and the danger—if she does not leap up, precisely at the precise moment if Promethea does not hurl herself upward, if the light does not smile, if she does not leap up to meet god's desire faster than even god himself, at the absolute speed of love—is that then it would be night, then my heart will be dashed against the heart of the earth like a child who falls from a roof to its mother's feet, like a dove struck down, the way an eaglet that left its aerie too soon, falls, like an egg, and will be crushed, if Promethea does not dash up immediately like a winged mare, like a saint inspired by passion, like the goddess, Humility, the one who does not know No, the almighty divinity of love, if she does not come rushing in her might and immediacy to meet my heart falling now toward her, like an apple that obeys the Earth's laws but orders the Earth: "Come! fall toward me the way I fall toward you," then if Promethea did not hold out her hands, the apple would be crushed, the child's blood would spill, in the center of the earth there would be a little spot, it would be night, love would be cold, if Promethea had not dashed forward when "Come!" was barely out of my mouth, in one leap, without hesitating, without thinking, had not loosed herself from the center of the earth, had not immediately torn herself from her time, her history, her laws, her country, the egg would have burst, the golden brains would have poured out, if Promethea had not, in that very instant, transformed herself into Humility, the great winged mare, and flapping her voluminous wings, her silvery mane standing on end, the banner slices through the air from the bottom up, she rises, she comes, she obeys, she takes the order, she picks up my heart, softly whinnying she comes in through the window, she puts my heart back into my breast. And she is there. I said: "Come!" And there was light, all the way inside my breast. And love in person in my arms. I gaze at her features for a long time. Those are indeed her features, this is she, this is the face of Come, the secret tender, mighty face of All-Is-Given, I bend over the rim of her eyes, I slip in, as I am, I don't know how, but burning hot and thirsty, into her soul, and as I am, I enter infinity with a sigh, as I am, dark and thirsty, love makes me fall into this water of thick and perfumed water, I am drunk, I feel wonderful, I want to fall again, again, I am falling into love itself, . . .

And then—how did this end? How does one end the infinite?

In the end Promethea was the one who went to make some fried eggs. To be done with the infinite? A little. Just a little? Because while they were eating their eggs they ate a little leftover infinity with them. That is what made them eat so absentmindedly. Cold eggs; but real ones. Remembering the fall. Or maybe still very slightly falling. And completely dazed I gaze in amazement at Promethea, I look at her and I see her close up and at the same time so infinitely distant, but the close up is so close that it is like distance exploded, and completely dazed I shut my eyes, I founder, it is too bright around me, I feel I need a sea to carry me to some shallower moment.

What happens: I let myself go to live in the depths, near the sources. I follow in the footsteps of every mystery. Rather than avoid things I don't understand I go that way on purpose. I want whatever happens to me by surprise. When something suddenly upsets me, I pause over it: I ask "why?" I live with shivers. I only want to live where I shiver. Never have I spent so much time so far so obscurely so deeply inside such storms. I dive in—thanks to Promethea. I go through her. I enter infinity by going through her.

I don't know how to explain. Promethea is a woman? Yes. Is a mare? Yes. Is also a Yes. Yes to all I want. To all? Yes. To all I want to pursue, to attempt, to experience. Yes. That is why when I go through her I come to infinity.

I was watching her, just now, eating eggs. I saw everything. I saw the light, the light as a veil. I saw the yellow of the egg yolk. I saw Promethea as she exists—for her own story, in her own person, and at the same time I saw her from the point of view of infinity, but I didn't manage to tell her that, because it took all I had just to keep myself ever so slightly together around a minuscule point of myself, my soul, my being only held onto the present by a wisp of Promethea's magical mane, with which I wrapped my gaze, otherwise I would have vanished far away, far, far away.

I said: I saw her from the point of view of infinity. I am not infinity. Yet I saw infinity. Sometimes one sees God. Seeing God is not impossible. It is Saying that is beyond our powers.

Or maybe beneath them? Yes, that is more like it: the best Saying can do as far as infinity is concerned is to call it God. I would like to create the true portrait of Promethea, which would have to be simple and double to be true.

First of all Promethea is a woman. I can describe her and I will do so. It will be hard, because she has a simplicity that defies description. But at the same time she is a heroine of infinity.

She will always be there.

But she is not always where she is. She is not far away but often I don't know where she is, in what city, what she is turning into and what shape she is taking.

She is always in transfiguration. In the morning I am enchanted, I watch her, I beg her "keep doing that! go on! go on," the sight of her thousand faces moves me. In the evening I have had enough, I am afraid, I suddenly cry out "stop! if I were sure you are a mare I would pull on your bridle until your lips bleed." But just for that, she is a child crawling out of the river on all fours and shaking with laughter.

Better to catch her when she wakes up.

In the morning I adore her because she lets herself be created. I waken the earth by caressing all its surfaces, and the earth hums to itself, still dreaming, sings its own awakening, awakens welling up in celebration, wakes up rejoicing, and turns into a river that flows between rocks, her face turned toward the sky, humming to herself.

She runs along . . .

All night long I run along behind her singing.

I call her: My Luminous Heart Who Goes Away in the Morning and at Night Comes Back to Sleep in my Breast.

She opens her right eye.

Immediately she starts thinking far away. I love her less. I love her even more.

What does she think about when she opens her right eye?

—About Beirut.

—About the caves at Lascaux.

—About the mystery of schools of fish: death has more trouble catching them all together.

I don't want to think about Beirut when I wake up. I want to keep on thinking about paradise, fruits, Promethea's arms, I want to forget my night's nightmares, I don't want to remember my day's nightmares, I want to wake up on the top of Mount Ararat and not leave my ark for one trouble-free hour.

Also I want to sing the day.

But Promethea is waking up in Lebanon. And I, now, where do I live? On what shores shall I write? Oh, my light, my real heart, my organs! My day breaks far from here I have to go to the school for love.

(I wonder: could I be jealous of Beirut?)

At school, discovery: having always imagined life to be absolute, two, god, and the desert. Suddenly to discover: no two without everything else. Promethea from every part of the world. I who wanted to believe that one times two was enough to be the world!

Another discovery: the more time one has the less of it one has. Time is reduced to days, days are reduced to minutes.

Nostalgia for days of minutes? For minutes of the past? The infinite minutes of dayless time? No.

Apprenticeship: unremitting labor in paradise so living it will be paradise. Slavery of paradise. Otherwise it is hell.

I go back to Promethea at the source: when she bubbles out of night's rock humming, running along her path, with her face to the sun. Transparent, undeterrable.

She does not understand the abyss. Does not guess how the abyss is jealous of the river.

Transparent: no bad thoughts?

Simple, frightening in her simplicity, threatening in her simplicity, in her transparence. How could the not-divided understand division?

Mysterious. Mysterious to herself. Does not know she is mysterious.

Lets herself go completely, throws herself at me as humbly as if I were divinely greater than she, or the sea.

That is how Promethea won H's soul, without taking it, by not taking it, giving herself boundlessly.

Does not consider the powers of her humility because she is truly so humble that she does not know she is humble.

So much more powerful than herself.

Survivor. Survivor from divine times. You are unconscious of yourself the way the earth is unconscious of itself.

She is incomprehensible. Inexplicable. Why at night does this sudden desire, a great black shiny violent foal, carry her away, cry out "I want you to split open my breast, I want you to set my heart free," want to offer her life to be drunk, want the knife in her breast, eat my heart, I want to be good things for you, your rice, your food, I want to be the apple between your teeth, take my life. Inexplicable. Why so impatient: when would I be able to offer to die for you?

Knows no other way of living than dying. Died of not being able to die. Never stretches out along the shores of night without having left a window wide open through which to throw herself toward God at the first sign that he wishes it.

"Do you want me to throw myself out the window?" she calls out. And God remains silent too. His only answer is the evening cool. Because he knows that Promethea is of the same ilk as Abraham. And I know: if I say "yes," she'll do it. How do I know that? I believe her. I believe everything she says. Sometimes when I talk I use words that are a little old, sentences from the day before, or I share with others thoughts that I have more or less tapped already. I let myself say things sometimes that are not perfectly fresh, but nonetheless still true enough that I don't run the risk of imposture. Sometimes, like most people I know, I speak not-quite. This is a thoughtless, fickle, superficial language, likely to flip over to its opposites, one that does not really care at all about what it says.

But Promethea cares carnally about what she says. Watch out for words with her! Because Promethea is the person who has not cut the cord binding words to her body. Everything she says is absolutely fresh. Comes straight from the flesh of her lungs, the fibers of her heart. She doesn't know any other way of speaking. That is why her words are few and fiery. And all her sentences are strong and young and incandescent, because they are caused by a convulsion of her whole earthly body. Promethea's thought is of quivering red lava. And all her remarks date from the beginnings of life. Even concerning details she is cosmogonic. She moves easily to the ends of the earth, the places where life takes on form or loses it.

Never will I be able to say: "If you want me to I will throw myself out the window." Never will I be enough of a believer to believe my own self. But Promethea has the incredible strength of believing herself. She is someone who has never betrayed herself. And I, I don't know how, slipping up on a few words that are too polite, too polished, I skid sometimes, I miss the point of what I meant to say, I miss the truth. Or is it maybe a question of weight? Because I am too light to stay in the depths of language, I rise to the surface, I have to struggle to dive back down. Whereas Promethea, thanks to her immense body that weighs its weight in truth, settles easily to the depths of herself, right next to her heart's lips. And she agrees with herself immediately. Maybe.

To tell the truth, I always feel I am slightly lying when I miss her with my words or consequently that I barely speak the truth. Every now and then I feel the cord between my belly and my words is absent. My flock is straying. But I pursue them in all honesty when I think they are truly too far afield.

Would I go so far as to put my own flesh on the line to vouch for my word? I don't know. That is why I ask Promethea not to ask me anything that would cost my imagination too much. I am willing to die like everybody else, but I know that if dying is necessary at least I want to profit as much as possible from life. That is why I beg Promethea to spare me the window ordeal. I am not lying: I am perfectly willing to die with you, Promethea, I mean: die well, slowly and magnificently, our golden gazes mingled, warmly and tooth to tooth, with extraordinary crimson satins at the windows, or even without any satin, but with time enough to imagine the whole sky as soft eyelids, and time enough to let the most beautiful the most final the most precise celebrations rise from my heart to my throat, I'm perfectly willing to do that, with infinite thinking and bloods uniting at our center—but I do not feel capable of Promethea's act. No window, no window for me! I am too much of an egoist. To lose living and dying in the same instant, that is beyond me. I concede: I insist, at least, on my death. I don't want to die without having really known it. I desire intensely what the process of dying will allow me to discover between worlds. This treasure and this reward are things Promethea renounces without a moment's hesitation. She dares to die absolutely. What is more, she does not live; she *has* her life, as her finest jewel. What is rare is that she has her own life so utterly at her disposal. And she only wants to give her dearest possessions. It is what she needs. This need is her very life. A woman of her word, that is to say a woman of her flesh, is what she is.

How do I know this?

I feel it. When I move my hands over her great dreaming belly, my fingers feel the delicate roots of words quivering.

—But when she asks: "Do you want me to jump out the window?" isn't she sure you will say no?

—She leaves it up to me. She opens the window for me. She forbids me to lie. I am free to say yes for fun. But no one is playing. She flings her life out the window of my heart.

—But there is no way she can believe you want that.

—She would like me to want it. She hopes that one day I will want it.

—Is she crazy?

—From our point of view, yes. But from God's, no. I try to look at her by entering into God's line of sight. Because it is clear to me that what makes Promethea so rare is her way of living every day on nature's scale, inside the seething of Creation. Every morning, she throws herself out the window into infinity. Sometimes she gets no farther than the end of the garden, which makes her cry. Because there are times when she manages to travel the whole world from Paris to India, and afterward, at the end of the afternoon, her body shimmering with roses, with golden glints, with dust, with sand and the tears of thirty countries, still she gallops on as far as the desert that comes after the world. And there, finally, it is her pleasure to swiftly raise a voluminous silk tent the color of twilight, where she spends the night dreaming great geographical dreams for the trips of tomorrows.

But those days when she only gets as far as a city, a beautiful one but too nearby and somewhat realistic, she despairs. She feels as utterly dismayed as the mouse who was condemned to move a pyramid. A momentary lapse. Because some other day she would get right to it, moving the pyramid if necessary, to make a nice neat desert again.

I read these pages to Promethea in person. And she did not recognize anything. And she said: I'm afraid.

—Why?

—You're making her like a god. You put her up there among the naive gods.

—She is one of the naive gods. That is why she is so fragile. Nowadays those gods have become extremely mortal.

—You don't mention that you are my river of honey.

—No. I myself can't make the picture of me that is in you. But maybe in my portrait of you my transparency can be seen.

—Stop, please. I miss you.

I miss you too, Promethea. While I am reflecting you, you flash whinnying past the window and I never even saw you vanish. By talking about you I lost sight of you. It is dark, I am alone. Wait for me in some country. I'll tidy up, I'll condense, take a short cut, here I come.

To finish up: Promethea is one of the rare creatures that is truly mortal. (Because we humans no longer know how to be mortal, none of us.)

A woman of profusion. Whom one word could kill.

If I said: yes . . .

Is it the kind of portrait this is that is bothering me? Maybe its the genre. Because Promethea can't be *seen,* not full-face, what I see therefore is not seen, for example, if I lean over the banisters to watch her gallop upstairs, her mane like a halo lighting the walls of the dark shaft, her eyes glowing so that even myopic me, I could find her in the darkest garden. How her soul burns just beneath the skin making her cheeks all crimson like a little girl flushed with joy can't be seen either. It's true that I began to make this portrait at first from so close up, eyes shut, by ear. And then I observed her from the side and from underneath and from the inner point of view located inside my breast far enough to the right that my heartbeats don't break the thread of my ruminations. And then, it doesn't look like Promethea springing up, it looks like . . . a written-down Promethea or a well-thought-out one—I don't know what you would call it, a Promethea digest, philosophicopromethea . . . I'm not happy with it.

Still, I'm afraid that if I changed genres today I would be deprived of the pleasure I have sniffing thoughts of Promethea and ruminating over them. I admit: I get some satisfaction from dreaming in the meadow when the magical mare is not there, my mouth full of grasses permeated with her spirited perfume, Fougueux. "I'm fine without you," I would go on savoring. Because Promethea's absence has a truly intoxicating taste; the whole meadow has the sweet smell of her skin.

Oh, Promethea, every trace of you smells so good! When I tell you "Go away, please," it is just to get a better whiff of you, sweet flesh loaf.

My odd sort of gluttony even wins out over my displeasure. Will I let myself have one last day in the solitary meadow? While the real Promethea goes to the real market, am I going to regurgitate and taste all over again the figurative Promethea?

(With these words I stop, because the moon is already

growing large in the rosy sky. I will continue when dawn comes.

Now it is the dawn of the one hundred and second day. I pick it up again.)

However:

Promethea goes to the market alone. She buys forty pigeons. She is going to clean them. Never careful how she spends.

But I am careful how I spend Promethea. I take thoughtful little tastes. I have the time it takes to do forty pigeons for my treat. I turn every flavorful tuft ten times around in my mouth:

—Why do so few people stand up for you? Why do so many people take fire from you. Take the warmth from your body, from your life, and leave? Yesterday, why did no one tell you thanks, but your creatures got all the praise?

Because they are so many people who take your fire. That is why they don't stand up for you. Because people don't give to the person they take from. Because people who take, take over. Don't know how to take well, don't know the secret of good taking, which is: if you take something, take it in, learn. If you take, discover the source: lean over the water and for an instant respect it. Gently respect its depth, its limpidity, before drinking. Then the water that is respected is even more refreshing, more caressing and spiritual.

But taking people swallow water without having loved it, swallow and aren't thirsty anymore, no more emotion, no more drive, swallow, wipe their mouths, and leave without reflecting, with souls arid as ever.

The water weeps, sometimes, water is a gift of tears. Someone has wept tears of love for us. And we wipe our lips thanklessly.

I swallow. I lick my lips. Promethea is in the kitchen. I don't know what she is doing.

I take another mouthful, thoughtfully. Time dawdles in my meadow:

—Why do so many people drink your tears and eat your fire. But so few stand up for you?

It is because your water is so crystal clear. There is no silvering on your soul. Leaning over you, one does not see one's reflection. Only your transparency.

It is because you are so simple. You lack perversities. There is something fishy about you. You are not two-faced. Faced with your simplicity, duplicity goes wild with exasperation.

You are a believer.

You are almost impossible.

You are such a believer: there is no room for demons anywhere near you. And so what do the people who come with their demons, those people, what do they do with their demons who can't stand the atmosphere around you? They have to keep them shut up in their kitchen, where they bark and piss angrily.

Because your goodness isn't good for everyone.

And pure air is poison for impure beings. Purity is not purifying. On the contrary . . .

All the same, I do know what she is doing, whether she is in the kitchen, in the streets of New Delhi, sweeping by in the clouds or deep in the newspaper.

She is spending a fortune.

One day, she has this vision of Ash descending the Nile in a royal galley, dressed in a costume whose beauty was a secret lost three thousand years ago. She sees it all, the secret is revealed to her. And while she is waiting to go to Egypt to the exact spot on the banks she dreamed of, she makes the costume she thought of. She runs off to Lyons, otherwise she would go to Calcutta. She cuts and pieces together moon silks that only survive in one workshop, where the last weaver who knows the secret of legendary fabrics is completing her dream. She wants to dress Ash in the last dress whose description merits two nights of storytelling. In her fever she thinks only about her work, she wants to give Ash a vision of a robe, she feels neither hunger nor cold, her soul is the Nile, she wants to carry Ash three thousand years ago, between her banks, she forgets to sleep, she dreams now in broad daylight, she sews up sections of orange river, she forgets to get dressed and when that evening arrives she is all undressed and out of breath, adorning Ash in the never-to-be-seen-again robe. And the one who never even had time to put on her panties was Promethea. (I'm telling this while she is downstairs and doesn't hear us. Because if she caught us she would fidget in shame. She would try to shut me up. And then? Maybe I would give in. Out of love. But maybe, out of another love I would refuse to shut up. And we would fight, the way we did once already, until there was hurt and anger and lying: "You don't love me, I know it. No it's you, yes it's you, yes it's me, who doesn't love me, that I don't love" . . . I can hear it.

More ruminating.)

I asked her, "do you know how different you are? From most?" She didn't know.

Because you don't make mistakes. You don't know where you are going. Yet you get there. And how do you get there? Simple, going straight ahead.

You want the sky, and up you climb, straight up.

You don't prove things. But you yourself are the proof.

In the battle between angels and demons we are secretly on the side of the demons; at best we don't take the demons' side, but we don't take the angels' side.

What does she do to be innocent? That is something, obviously, she doesn't know, because she doesn't do anything.

She is a creature from before History.

She protests it's not so.

—You are also a creature from after.

But myself, when I was born there was History all around, everywhere, crammed full of refuse and corpses, in the cities, in the countryside, and it was almost impossible to clear a path through to the mountain. Up above life would have been different. Promethea's cradle caught in a bunch of grass on top of Ararat where it stayed. That is why she is more optimistic than I. Mud never blocked her view.

That is the whole difference between us.

Because if the cops stop her because she doesn't have her license plates, she can tell the truth, which is that she never bought them, that's all, and they don't arrest her, because how would they arrest her, her, the doe who has just been transformed into a woman, a quarter of a mile from the Route de la Reine, whose skin still smells like a doe in autumn, wet from the forest. But me, they would arrest me immediately, because I'm guilty, I know it, I am guilty of things she is innocent of, I am guilty because I know it, I know it, I am guilty of knowing I am guilty, but she doesn't know, and even the cops can feel it, smell it in the damp mossy fragrance rising from her eyes . . .

The mystery: even if you had committed a crime you would be innocent. Your soul is made of innocence. Does that mean you never do anything wrong? I think so. The worst you can do is "act badly," a child's crime, because you always act with your child's heart: I meant that you never commit any deed with an adult's hard heart, a heart with authority.

—I hope you're not saying good things about me?

—Actually, I'm describing your failings.

I know things you do with that child's heart. You forgot the little old watercress lady who had saved her ten bunches of watercress for you. But you paid for that emotionally all the next week, and you will keep on paying for a long, long time, until the gods are willing and you find your old watercress lady again. She has still not come back!

And then: some other child sins. Because you grew up in the heart of the lonely Gaste Forest, with its delightful gentle weather, until the morning you suddenly knew you wanted to leave it, and immediately, forever, and you knew so intensely that you wanted to go take on the big world, and with no more ado, that very hour you take your leave, your mother weeps, hoofs stamp the old ground feverishly, and you are already far in the future, racing off with moans of joy, not looking back and you leap full speed ahead toward the wonderfully beautiful world. And you never went back.

And there are all the old women, small or medium-sized, that you leave behind weeping, with your child's heart, racing past them at such a lively gallop that the cloud of dust your hoofs raise hides them from your eyes. You could slow down. You could phone them at the end of the day. And plenty more things you've done that I've forgotten. Because you paid for them with huge tears that make your eyes vast and trembling.

And there are all the failings you never pay for with tears. Your failings due to greatness. Your great lack of smallness. Your divine lack of imagination. You don't know that most people are small. You have no respect for their smallness. You mistreat them: you treat the bad guys like the good. You treat people who enjoy being enemies like friends.

What puts demons off the most is the friendship angels have for them. You don't understand that.

You have no pity. Only trust. One more failing.

You never take revenge. Not that you know nothing about wanting vengeance. But because you always have a new palace to build. And you don't want to waste time destroying. But the human mob, avenging and avenging, wastes its life on vengeance, wants to have revenge on you who never take the time to get your revenge too. While you are building palaces, people fell and fall, and resent you for not wasting time like everybody else.

You offend them (rightly) because you don't offend them.

Sins that your virtues are. You act (virtuously) in defiance of our world.

But perhaps your greatest failing is to do stingy people

wrong by believing them generous? To shame the jealous by believing them incapable of jealousy?

But is that maybe your greatest strength also? Sometimes the brilliance of your belief dazzles demons for a second. During this second, destruction is suspended.

But then it starts up again worse than ever.

The demons only want there not to be, not to be.

And Promethea, neck outstretched, quivering flanks, soul longing after stars, wants there to be, to be.

You are not the other.

—Are you crying? Don't cry. I love you for these failings. I love how you smell of the primeval forest. I love your not knowing good and evil. I love your ignorance of half the world. I am delighted that you don't know your own power. If you knew it perhaps you would never do anything again.

As I write this I am smiling at the thought that Promethea, when I hand her this paper mirror, will not recognize herself. These days I look a bit lost—and perhaps younger—because there is no mirror in this house. That gives me a strange feeling of being without myself. But I am constantly with Promethea, even when I don't know where she is, whether in the kitchen or in the garden, or . . . Even when I'm not thinking about her. Because the house is completely magical these days. I feel the fire of Promethea's soul warming my hands. The air inside the house is lush and green. Our thoughts go softly back and forth in the same meadow, meeting in the staircase, embracing with a smile, our silences flow together in matching rhythms between the same banks.

Night comes.

—I've been in touch with you all day, Promethea, do you understand that?

—It's love.

—But sometimes in the midst of love there are wars, walls, sometimes there are foreign languages separating love, a crowd of strangers, sometimes one can pass by each other at a distance of years, centuries, histories. It's hard to hear, we call each other, we have to yell, break through, work so hard.

Sometimes one is inside, the other outside. One inside a memory to which she alone has the key, the other alone on the Moon, her body galled because no one came with her, and through the sore, unwanted passersby can enter.

Love is so often scoured, invaded, spoiled.

And then love thinks of love.

But today I didn't have to think about you. We were together inside the same real dream. We germinated inside the curving pearly shell of the same Great Egg. I wonder which of our stars laid it for us.

Today I am angry with Promethea. Because once again she has spent everything. She spent us. She gave everything we had to the little Gypsy who knocked on the door. She gave him all our time. I made a scene about it:

You get up inside your warm house, you walk through your warm house, you go to the window of the warm house, it's cold and damp outside, there is a little boy, weather-beaten and sad, wandering around outside, in front of the house, and you race out of the warm house, you cry: I want to do something for you, little boy, I want to help you, you run around and cry, outside, and inside the house is alone, your house is shivering, your house wants to sleep or grow old, your house wants to explode.

Oh, You are my Child, but I don't want to be your mother. You are my dreamer Child, I want you to dream, but I don't want to be your night.

I missed you. It's not tomorrow that I want you. It was today, this very day, this very past day. I did not kiss you today, I will never kiss you, not ever not tomorrow. I am dead for the tomorrows. Tomorrow I am not yet born . . . (But tomorrow do I already love you?)

Day 132. Three weeks of wind and cold.

It is not yet daylight when Promethea wakes me up in
tears: "I dreamed that I woke up and you weren't there, you
weren't in the bedroom, you weren't in the house and there
was no trace of you anywhere as if you had never been here,
the house was full of echoes and empty of enchantment, as if I
had only dreamed your presence, I went out, there was no
one in the world, I wandered, I could not bear the icy weight
of my whole life bearing down on my chest, and I started to
die without being able to cry."

—"I dreamed they woke me up to tell me that you were re-
ported missing. In fact you were not in the bedroom, but the
house was full of traces of you, the air was green and lush,
there were hairs from your mane on the curtains. I was sure
you were not dead. Just a little lost. I guessed you had wandered off, perhaps in some faraway country. Hurriedly I got
my things together, in a twinkling I went off to look for you,
it was still night when I arrived in Vietnam. If I don't find her
here, I said to myself as I plunged into jungles of ruins, I'll go
to Tibet as fast as I can."

But we couldn't figure out which dream engendered
which.

Often some fear coming from where we are rooted assails
one of us.

Once, at table, Promethea, trembling all of a sudden without saying a word, looked at H, as if she were bending over
the corpse of a little girl. H took her in her arms and said:
"Don't be afraid."

Promethea cried out: "You know how frightened I am,
I'm frightened." And neither of them knew what the other

was afraid of. But the room was full of a soft wet fear that came up to the edge of the table.

I don't know, however, what to be afraid of anymore. There is nothing to be afraid of in our garden. Maybe that is why we are sometimes so frightened. We no longer know how to be ill-fated.

There are new terrors growing in our garden. I already smell their aroma, but I don't recognize their flowers yet.

The same peace gives birth to Felicity one day and to Dread another. The season of new terrors. Bunches of hell are growing at the foot of the Tree of Life.

They spend the hundred and fourth day fleeing violently toward each other. Why?

Because nothing keeps them from contemplating, staring, loving, approaching, touching, embracing each other,

taking, marrying, merging, advancing into each other, stumbling into the other, plunging into the other, going under, drowning,

for nothing anymore, nothing separates them, there is time, there is space, there is day and night, there is body, there is blood,

then, everything that does not separate them begins to separate them, everything they share and everything separating them inseparably joins them, and everything that brings them closer and everything that says yes to them,

then a great No comes up out of the north, and begins to blow in the garden, around the bed and even into their eyes

And they spend all that day step by step assessing and excessing in minute detail the almost nothing separating them, one centimeter of difference in all, one immeasurable centimeter, an infinitesimal bit of infinity, infinity.

Because the one hundred and fortieth day was so sweet . . .

And there was the fight in the plains of Médoc. All day

long they fought. They hurt each other as much as is possible without hating. But love fainted dead away.

And the reason for the fight?

Bedreddin Hassan thought he would die for not having put pepper in a cream pie. That was during the hundred and twentieth night. And H thought she would lose Promethea for a smile that wouldn't come on some damned dry and dusty road.

And Promethea thought she could never come back because she had already gone in the opposite direction for an hour.

And H thought their eternal youth was lost because a whole month had passed without one of their most beautiful words being uttered. And the thirty-first day the word came back to the ark and landed, wings still trembling from the expedition, and landed on Promethea's lips: "Hallelujah!"

But Promethea thought that they were being approached by some death because H no longer remembered their first forest, or their first spring, under their first tree. Or the cold? Or the warmth given? Or Promethea's shining face above her face. And for the first time Promethea was the one frozen. Until finally H remembered the cedar tree. Then the field. Then the sky. And there in the sky love's first face was shining.

Because they sometimes took shortcuts through death to find themselves more alive again.

I don't want to forget. I would like so much not to forget the one I was. I want to keep the taste of solitude, I want to keep the soul I had for solitude, I don't want to lose the being I had for poverty. I am so rich now and from this moment on, so rich everyday, I am afraid to forget how lucky it is to be wealthy. I am afraid of losing the keen joy of sudden wealth, I am afraid of losing infinite wealth in poverty, I want to keep both the faint and the flamboyant wealth, I want to be afraid of forgetting, I am afraid of losing that fear too: everything is so equally sweet, so smiling and peaceful in the Garden,

Quick, a storm! A knife! Kill me a little.

—Would you really be willing to die for me?
—Aren't I already dying for you? by living for you?

And some days are as suddenly cruel as a caliph's whim. But that is because it is all lived out so close to humanity's savage heart. In this region everything is so sensitive that a grain of pepper could blow up the earth. One little silence and it's death. One spoonful of light spilled from eyes: a new life. A quiver of the nose: space gapes open, the earth falls to the bottom of the universe.

Often it is hell: a missed paradise, paradise that might have happened, paradise right at hand, it is there, just in front of the house, the paradise that stays there, brilliant possibility, absolutely inaccessible, surrounded by its transparent wall, always lost again, the paradise nearly gained.

It is hell, I grab happiness by the hem of her dress, and I am not strong enough to hold onto it, happiness moves on, as if I did not exist for her, the dress slips through my fingers, its silk caressed my fingers.

It is really always paradise.

On the hundred and forty-sixth day a monstrous unknown anger came and glued itself to H's skin. Anger of monumental dimensions, an anachronistic sort of drunken anger, not divine, that she could not succeed in pulling off. The whole day was played out in spite of her in an epic register that was completely out of place in the bedroom reigned over by Promethea's grand, wild, and familiar style. And the one who suffered from ridicule was H:

—Don't you think it's nice like this—Promethea began in a warm voice, and she tasted how nice it was with the point of her kitten tongue, tasted with her tongue in and out, tasted the edge of the day, delicately lapping it with no trace of anxiety—how nice it is—she was asking me—hidden in the warmth of our comforter, and the comforter was all-embracing, spreading a milky warmth all over the place, spreading thick clouds of tender warmth over their bodies and onto the river, and over all the waters and over the whole course of her existence, and the day all warm with color came flowing through the window,

and this is how, as if she were carried without a jolt on the bosom of a giant dream, Promethea made her entrance into the little 146th day, smoothly, with no break from nighttime, passed from dark warmth to warmth the color of rose tango,

—don't you think it's nice like this, she went on tasting, her eyes nestling, her big body small and motionless in a giant feathered hollow,

seen and heard by H, her eyelids up, her eyes naked, watching Promethea's great body scarcely rocking inside her transparent shell, hearing, helmet up, soul at a high pitch and trembling with the desire to plunge up to the hilt into the day, into time's beating heart, soul trembling with the need to run at the world, to pounce on the trace of mysteries, hearing, throat filled with fiery cries held back, held back, the slow stirring of words along Promethea's calm lips.

—don't you think—there underneath like two little twins in a kangaroo's pocket—she was still savoring, egglike, knees under her chin, breastless, bellyless, sexless, rocking back and forth between two times, and the day licking gently at her shell. All wrapped up in a great warm eyelid. And H, her spear right next to the bed, her gallantry annoyed, her soul in the clear, didn't answer:

—I don't want to be nice like that.

She did not shout it. She did not say: I don't like that niceness. She thought that. She burned that.

Why not say it? one thing or the other?

She didn't say:—I don't want to sleep together in day's down pocket. I want to plunge into the day at a gallop, I want to scour every hour of the day, I want to go straight through the heart of every hour, I want to chew time up, I want to taste every drop of blood, I want to drink some of all the day's tastes, I want to hunt down a god to his last lair, a god? what's this? god—yes—I say god because that is what I call the being that will lead me alive, to the final hour, the black, glowing, wildly white hour that burns at the center of time, the hour in whose bosom everything is intensely alive, everything violently in the process of living itself, the hour of passion in which everything that lives is shriekingly, amazingly alive, everything alive fights over and rips itself from the earth, from paths, from footsteps, rips itself and carries itself away from peace, from succession, the hour of war when everything alive ventures right into the face of death, right into the face of life,

and that time when everything that takes place comes right back to life, when everything starts again endlessly, is where I want to go exhaust myself with living, but it is somewhere I cannot go alone, because one can give oneself one's own death, but no one can give herself such a fierce, powerful, lioness life.

Alone, such a life would kill me instantly. One cannot keep it without dying or wanting to extinguish it. It must be passed on, entrusted, given back. I cannot get there or stay there for a while unless a god accompanies me. And I would like for the god to be you.

And Promethea was a great woman who woke up without any fuss, without suspicions, without transposition. Thinking calmly about eggs and tea to start things off.

And H did not say:

—I want to be aflame, I want to kiss you, I want to put fire in your heart and to fling myself into your heart, I want to feed my fire with a tender piece of your heart. I would like to dare smash your shell, and I would like to frighten your eyes with the sight of my blazing heart, I want to bare you, to fling you into the raging heart of my day, I want to squeeze you in my flames. It is fire, fire that I like. I'm cold. It's just warm here, lukewarm. I'm hungry. My fire writhes with hunger in my breast. My fire wants to lick your breasts. I'm thirsty. My fire wants to suck the salt of your tears.

That is what she thought. Not what she said. Because it was Sunday. Because Promethea was not yet born. All folded up on herself inside her big transparent shell she teetered on the light, on the edge of day's crater. Did not hear love growling in her gut. It was the day for Hatching. Because Promethea was dawdling on the edge of day and singing the song about rolls ("My brown bread roll, my cumin roll, my poppyseed roll, my Tibetan roll," etc.).

Tomorrow, she thought, brooding over the egg woman with her naked eyes, I'll explode in burning words, tomorrow I'll attack you with love, first thing in the morning, I'll graze you with my spear.

She said nothing. But her silence was so ardent that Promethea felt it blow across her eyelids like a sirocco. And suddenly she leapt out of the kangaroo pocket just the way she was, without a shell, without any superficial skin, featherless, absolutely naked as never ever and never again. So sincerely naked that the silence inside H's breast subsided. She burned less. She could smile. She put her helmet away in the closet for the day.

Promethea's exercise class (exercises that last twenty-seven minutes to the tune of Jane Fonda's *Workout*):

Start, top: She is gone. Let her go away without following her, without going with her to the door, one, without running to the balcony to see one second longer her shiny little helmet, two, without shouting to the sun: "don't set, come down and get me, I'm afraid of the dark," three, without taking the car to catch her at the end of the road, begin arm movements, eight times, without spilling more tears than all the children in the world, legs spread apart, without falling to the bottom of life the way a corpse falls, seven, eight, hold still, breathe, without your eyes latching onto the watch hands to avoid sinking into the abyss, stretch, pull in your stomach, squeeze your buttocks, without gloomily celebrating this first pain, it burns, smile, mane flying, back straight, without crossing the terrible primal deserts again, without wanting to die a little so this dull burning of the heart will stop for a second, change legs.

Let her go, half an hour, as if she were only going off in a dream, to run an errand. Jog in place, again, where?

To the drugstore, for example. Twist. As if half an hour of such effort were not endless. Keep it up. As if half an hour had not gone by in the very instant she left. As if half an hour were not the chance for a hundred fatal accidents, time for arrest, time for torture, time for treachery, time for loyalty, time for the left side, pull, pull. Nineteen minutes ago her head was right here where I could see it and since then I have lost a child, I have wept on her bed, I have sniffed her scent still alive still how long still a few more hours her scent surviving, I kept her here a little longer with her scent, I held onto the first days full of their thousands of days to come, the first days of quivering, the first large undiluted days, days with an absolutely naked cloudless sky, days of arrival, nothing but arrival keeping on arriving, I relived our future lives fluttering along the edge of the first days open and unblinking upon the naked sky, I relived roaring laughter months, still fearless exultations already sweetly tenderly greedy for themselves, raptures watching them congratulate themselves ever so slightly, I relived the first times, the next times, the imprudent times, and the joyfully stingy times, all those and the ones after, the fourth, the happiest, the least yet somehow most burning, and I relived the last right up to this moment and this one I am still reliving with a flat belly, twenty-three minutes already,

legs bent, heels to buttocks, kick, kick, keep the rhythm— I hang onto it by the still-damp edge of her scent, now the abdominals. I can't, my stomach hurts too much, I can only relive, I can live nothing except this reliving, and when the scent is gone, I'll die, my head on my arms, knees crossed, I'll rest—

How long does a scent live on? She's been gone for twenty-four minutes.

And ever since I keep breathing everything I lost, I feel the child in my belly still, just about to leave me,

And for twenty-six minutes I live in no time or space,

It is getting too hard for me, I'm stopping. I quit.

What bothers me is that this is for beginners.

What consoles me is that afterward I'll do the cooking so she will come back. Because after all, even if some day there is an hour that is really endless, if I want to end it, there is always death.

But that is not part of exercising.

Now I myself would like to confide something very violent that happened one morning this week, in the darkest eroticism, I mean in a burning and painful obscurity of soul, with the soul in a state of raw nerves so that every word, every thought that brushed past me made me cry out in pain. But I think it is too hard to talk about this directly, from inside myself where these events that were so obscure, so faint, and yet as staggering as hurricanes of the soul. For three days I have been trying to get near the turbulent heart of the maelstrom, but I cannot do it, I push myself back, I climb, I descend, I climb back, I cart my notebooks around from east to west, from north to south. This morning I went down full of decisiveness, prepared, armed with seven ballpoint pens seven notebooks, and rather than laying the enemy who chases me away out on the page, I went and pulled up some bindweed, thinking "this bindweed is keeping me from writing." Until my hands were full of blisters.

Enough! I'm afraid. I want to pull back. I want not to pull back anymore.

I went back up. I shut the windows firmly. I beg the great sun not to light up anything more than the feverish morning setting my spirit on fire. Let the rest of the week be dark.

I begin.

I have to talk about myself by taking the necessary distance. That is why I prefer to leave the bedroom. I come back: H returns, trembling and shaky and dark as the shadow of a windblown willow. And yet no wind in the bedroom. And Promethea? Sitting. Serene. Like a queen in a dream. Motionless. Just a great peaceful breathing. But H feels her soul bend beneath a cold and harsh breeze. Don't show it. First thing is not to show it. Because she says to herself that this cold that is crushing her will go away, go away, maybe.

She feels like a stranger to herself, as much a stranger to herself as on coming out of a very intense dream, one stronger than herself, stronger than the day, a dream in which something bad has happened to her. And she is still crying at the end of the morning. Because sometimes the dream crushes the night before and takes over an entire day. Only another dream can drive it away.

She feels changed into something else. Because what she feels right now she herself never would have felt. What does she feel? Bad pain: that is a pain she hates and that hates her. Hand to hand they fight with their nails and threatening glances.

The fight began when Promethea apparently unsuspecting calm Promethea, normal it would seem, Promethea like always, Promethea without treachery or suspicion it seemed, her breath even and eyes bright as ever, or eyes maybe a little brighter, a little more burning it seemed, but her mouth apparently confident, her lips firm and facing straight ahead, without warning, Promethea suddenly announced the visit of her three nephews, and so

—So?

—So, there are three of them. One more therefore. Or one too many. Because there are only enough beds in the house for two. Therefore. That's it. Therefore there is one extra nephew. Yes.

So?

So that was when H began to feel some sort of wind blowing on her bones. At first she did not understand where the wind was coming from. Then she felt that it was coming from Promethea's words.

What was Promethea saying? It was as if she had brought her a delicious raspberry tart and at the first mouthful her tongue, her palate had been surprised by the taste of aloe spreading into her throat, all the way to her vocal cords and she couldn't even spit it out. The bitterness had saturated her mucous membranes, and already her soul was bitter and her eyes gone dark with anguish. Bitterly astonished she didn't spit didn't cry didn't even make a face. Trying first to wait it out.

—And the tart?

That was a metaphor. But not entirely: because H really felt the taste of fruit from the morning conversation turn into a bowl of bile. But the tart, I put it down in place of what Promethea said, which I'll summarize: what she said more or less, I think I remember, or maybe she didn't even say it because it was so obvious for her—Promethea—was that she would sleep with the Extra, and how the nephew would sleep with her, and how the nephew would sleep among her, and how the one among the three would be chosen with whom she would sleep among his body, and how the three candidates, how one of them, how he would win out, and then what a victory, what defeats, what a reward, what a night, and that was when H wanted to escape, do something, wake up because she had the sensation of having fallen into a treacherous, poisoned sleep, not even her own, someone else's sleep in which dreams that were too narrow, like cages, closed in upon her and squeezed her soul until it was smothering, but she could not get out, unfortunately, it was really into herself that she had fallen and she managed, painfully, to escape the little cage, twisting her soul and skinning her heart, only to find herself inside another cage just as narrow and evil and, to top it all off, magic, because she possessed the property of shrinking narrower and narrower and narrower until she felt like vomiting her own heart.

—All that just for a nephew? —Yes.

That is why it is so hard to tell. Because the smallness of the cause is so disproportionate to the cosmic devastation of the effect.

Devastation?

Yes: it made H feel she would do best to stay away from the window because with such a storm inside her being she could suddenly lose her balance and fall out rather than sinking down into the interior of her person.

And as if she had fallen from the pinnacle of culture, at the end of the evolution of the species, a hundred thousand years lower or worse, and now was roaming a jungle in which, moreover, she found certain satisfactions, growling almost shamelessly, though at first with some discretion, because she no longer knew exactly where she stood with Promethea. And she no longer was sure of who Promethea was, behind her facade.

As for her, every sense was sharpened. She heard in the distance and in anticipation. She heard: rustling leaves and sheets in the darkness of some impending starless night, little feet rubbing on large thighs, little groping fingers all over the large body stretched out in a thicket of pillows, the wild gong of a pealing heart swinging in her giant breast. (Because in the jungle her inner dimensions were superhuman. Inside she seemed to grow wider and deeper, a bottomless pit.)

She saw: a little dwarf man climb a mountain soft as butter leaving his footprints and handprints all over her buttocks, on her belly, on her thighs, trampling, polluting, plunging his hands into the cream and licking his fingers. And she saw: the mountain just letting it happen, asleep? Seemingly asleep. But letting herself be pressed, modeled, kneaded, gone all over, explored, and her earth quaking ever so slightly.

And she? back and forth at the foot of the mountain, in a

rage, seeing red, feeling anger like powerful electricity race to the end of her paws, pacing up and down the room and growling around the bed, and bit by bit finding some furious pleasure in this anger, in this pain, in this flood of annoyance, until all of a sudden she announces to Promethea:

—"I don't want you to sleep with your nephew."

Voluptuously dumbfounded to hear herself let out such a naked, such a shameless sentence, one so incompatible with human culture, rights and dignity, with the ideal of self, the respect for freedom, with generosity, stunned to discover voluptuousness in indifference to reason, intoxicated with shamelessness, injustice, the scent of new, bitter, breathless passions. She was in the process of loosing instincts that could have remained unknown to her forever: she was in the process of discovering the existence of egotism, of the merciless struggle for possession. And it wasn't bad. It was wildly delicious. It was exhilarating. It was good.

It was incredible in the bedroom. (Though not in the jungle.) Which is why Promethea hesitantly asks her if she is joking.

—Not at all—she growls, and her icy teeth sparkle in earnest.

I don't want any human whatsoever to touch you. She says, sinking her gaze unflinchingly into Promethea's trembling, moist eyes.

—But. Promethea murmured, uneasy, because torn between any number of feelings—but. But that's—that's . . . jealousy? But. You can't be (jealous) of a child?

Then H felt the wind blow three times as hard and all the jungle creak and groan, and the temperature of her passions went up, up, and all her body dilating as if her blood and her marrow were going to erupt.

Because what she just couldn't stand was that Promethea stay up there in the cool, quiet, cultivated, kindly, innocent world while she wandered around in her fiery forest. Because there are some sufferings that give pleasure, but others make you suffer. And maybe this was jealousy, this suffering that was giving her so much satisfaction and brought her, for example, the joy of wanting to kill, and so if this was jealousy, that was a desirable and imposing suffering. Because it gave her the strength to want to do something she would never have believed she could want to do, want, desire, delight in doing.

And what's more, she felt she would kill, she could kill, yes, she certainly would end up killing someone, she really felt there would be no other way to put out the fire that was consuming her jungle, except by pouring blood on it. And as to whom she would kill, it might be Promethea—or maybe herself, since she had already begun to murder herself a little . . .

But the thing that made her suffer, simply suffer, joylessly, not grandly, suffer with hunger, cold, and loneliness, was that Promethea would not lose paradise, never even thought it could be lost, did not even imagine that H could lose it, can have lost it, can want to lose it, want to carry pleasure to its satisfaction by fire, by blood, by pain, want to drink tears, and want to eat her, her Promethea, yes, bite her, cut her throat, consume her, yes, die from the need—want to punish her for her innocence, want to accuse her of innocence, condemn her for innocence, make her suffer a thousand pains to teach her for being ignorant of guilt, to teach her the terrible taste for cruelty, to make her feel the terrible delights of primal suffering, to teach her something about hell.

What sent her hurtling from her jungle into hell's cauldron, was that Promethea did not see the wind from her words bend her soul to the ground, did not see the flames consuming her bones, at the idea that a little dwarf man would eat her butter and drink her milk and press his little lips and his little penis on her mountainsides and even, maybe, make her quiver with tiny pleasures?

—Oh, Promethea, she doesn't say, wake up! Don't you see me burning?

Great flames wrapped around her. It was a relief. She blew on them herself to make them burn higher.

She already heard Promethea tell her in a voice cascading from the heights:

"We are innocent."

She already had time to see the tiny man reach the shoulder of the mountain by hanging onto her breasts.

And it was only then that she finally had the good fortune to be consumed.

I'll never have you enough. It is torture. It is luck.

I love you too much, I love you illegally: I love you truly. I love you when I didn't love you yet.

I fight over you with your mother: you go through me every morning to get to the day. You sleep and dream in my womb.

I create dawn for you. I open the world. I open the genital curtains so the light will come and kiss you.

I will never forgive you for everything you did when I did not yet exist.

Your past is not past. Your past surrounds me. Your past is present for me. How could I forget it? One only forgets one's own past. Now your memory is me.

I wonder if yesterday you were already Promethea? I think so. You were already her yesterday and the same today: the one who gives herself, Promethea run wild. That is why I hate you, why I love you.

She wants all of Promethea.

—I'm all yours.

—No. From the moment of your birth until I was there I still don't have you.

The only thing she could have altogether, the only thing

the only one still whole would be death, will be death.

Oh, Promethea, I am pursuing you to your first newborn cry, to your last death rattle.

The enigma of this love, this rage: it is because Promethea gives herself so truly wholly that I want her *even more*: I want everything she gives me, but it is not enough. I want to take also. And so how can one take when all is given? I also want what she cannot give me, what she does not know she has, what she has no more, what she is no more.

I do not want to *content* myself with what you give me, even if it is all you have. I want *more*. I want what you do not have the power to give me, I want to extract your secrets, things you don't know. I will never be contented, thank god!

—Clouds still, pages full of aberrations, winds, vertigo. But then the notebook calms down.

It is going to be pleasant.

Because deep in the heart of the excited universe, lies a little land of flesh, a little kernel of sweet soft mellow permanent warmth, the immortal animal, love: this body that is attached to this body, this body that pursues itself in the other body. I am attached to you through your organs, your body is part of my body, my flesh is necessarily graced with your flesh.

Warning: then comes a certain disorder in the notebooks. That is why I will no longer constantly put down what day it is. I want to leave a little of this disorder in homage to Promethea.

Promethea makes a distinction between sad order, sad disorder, poetic disorder, and the order of disorder.

She is poetically disorganized.

I want to tell the truth, without pride or modesty.

She asked me: Why do you love me?

—Because you never put the top back on the toothpaste.

—Because you pronounce "à tout hasard": Atouttazzar, who is one of my favorite pharaohs.

—Because you push yourself to extremes. Because yesterday you went farther than you could, and suddenly there was not even the least bit of strength left to pick you up. Down on your knees, under the world, you were struggling to get up.

—Because when you feel the end of one of your lives coming you find the strength to make your Tree of Dreams come true. To do this you follow the instructions in your books of sacred recipes: first dream the magical tree, the tree of trees, the total tree, the dream-bearing tree, the tree never seen before. To do this produce Arabia with mountains, oasis, and deserts. Run all over the land like in the tale of the 728th night to find the twenty-eight fruits, the hundred birds, and the six hundred branches; go through all the regions of the land to find each fruit in its garden, each tree in its orchard, each bird in its own nest; make the sixty trips required to bring together all the dreams that make the exact tree.

Other people go to the supermarket.

Mane flying, tracking down a dream, galloping, without letting the dream slip from view, making, making the unique tree come true, the tree that looks like a woman.

Other people buy easy fir trees, trees that look like mass-produced fir trees.

The strength to produce a tree of art is not one I have.

—Because you ask me: "When you say that Promethea makes a dream tree and that she goes all the way to India to find silks, and when you see perfectly well that I'm only making a Christmas tree, aren't you disappointed by the difference?"

—But what I write is indeed what is real. Wouldn't you go to Calcutta tonight for me?

—I would.

—Wouldn't you give up Calcutta for me?

—I'd give it up.

—Isn't it harder nowadays to discover the inner India than to go to Calcutta?

But the secret is perhaps merely that you are happy in my house (you love me). You don't find fault with me (you love me).

That's not an explanation? It's an answer.

I want to say some simple things about Promethea. That is the most difficult and most dangerous thing to do. Promethea is the simplest person I know.

—You think I'm too simple?

—I think you're very daring. Ordinary people are complicated. It's easy and comfortable to stay complicated.

I am afraid that if I say simple things about Promethea she won't be visible anymore.

Promethea's soul is a crystal tree.

Is what I am saying complicated? No. What I am saying is precisely very simple. After we fell out of the dream tree we were so twisted when we picked ourselves up again that now simple things seem complicated to us.

Anyone who knows that calling a white egg white risks causing the egg to seem to disappear along with the one calling it white and the whole visible world, will understand me. Does it seem, then, that I want Promethea to be visible?

—A little. I realize that this is an impure desire of mine. Love makes it enough for me to look at her in a delicate silence. It is adoration that makes me want to show her a little. In my everyday adoration I try to be slightly clever, I call her "a just cracked white egg," I talk about her, and I cloud her secret with the shadow of my words. I am afraid that if I say only the simple, true things about Promethea no one will understand me.

And the language is old too, the words are tired of defending their meaning. When the word "courage" was young it would have braved a thousand deaths without ever belying itself. But now, anything goes for courage, it goes so far as to let itself be used to describe cowardice.

To make a simple, faithful portrait of Promethea I would have to have ginger, for example, and shallots, along with spices' distinctness, the cook's tenacity, her proud modesty, hours of vigil spent on perishable things. If I could successfully describe Promethea cooking, would something of her mystery be captured there perhaps? In the kitchen, unlike writing, there are no synonyms. Each element in a harmonious dish is necessary and irreplaceable. Cooking according to Promethea is an art as superhumanly generous as that of producing a madly beautiful play in the theater the way it should be done. Madly beautiful? Because cooking and theater are mad arts: they are the arts of making things come true in reality that dreams only desire in dreams. No, no: they are the arts of making dreams true in reality. I mean of creating in reality things dreams only let themselves desire because they know that as dreams they cannot come true. And they are tragic arts: because their works have something of the nature of dreams: last only for a day or at the most a thousand and one nights. I am not brave enough. If books were edible would cooking them up be my quiet passion?

Theater, cooking, those are the great dreams that Promethea makes spring forth into the midst of reality. The dishes she perfects are as delicious as fantastic tales. At night she feeds me with subtly spiced dreams. And the dreamwork is a condensation of minutely detailed flavors, yet there is no metaphor. The alchemy of tastes. Promethea is absolutely strict as far as that science is concerned. And so I have to eat with intelligence and integrity. But when she asks me to help her make sauce for the soybeans, something so regal for something so poor. I see that this will take twenty-one gestures, seven spices, including ugly garlic, night ginger, and day ginger, I beg her to do without me. Such prodigious zeal seems beyond my means. But Promethea never hesitates over hard work. In the kitchen she prepares dishes with chivalrous reverence, no omissions, no confusion. There is a twelfth-century air of courtliness reigning around all the different ingredients. Under Promethea's leadership we have a taste of God. While I put together these last lines she is in the process of inventing a dish able to transport anyone who eats it to Baghdad, on the second mouthful.

When we returned from Baghdad (where we spent a night containing thirty-one days, and fruit stalls and flower stalls on the thirty-first night), this morning I continued confiding in Promethea.

Then she wrapped herself up completely in a long, very long, silence that left only her eyes showing, thinking, sparkling more than ever—because there were still some leftover Arabian lights in them. And over this silence, she grumbled:

—What you are doing. It's—the portrait of what is divine in human beings. The portrait of the divine spark in humans. Now you're smiling!

—Not everyone has a spark.

—I, in fact, believe this spark is in everyone.

—I can't share your belief. But it makes me happy that you have it. That is why I love you.

—It's—like Shakespeare when he created the portrait of Falstaff.

—I wouldn't paint that portrait. I don't know how to love those I don't love. My love is limited, boring, lazy. I only love lovable things. . . . A spark is too small. I only see the big fires. If you burned less I wouldn't want to come near you. I want your fire. I am only an Ash. I need some great woman to rise up from my cinders. I don't love Creation, including all its creatures. God's love is indifferent. Mine is a narrow, elective passion. Thank God you are more the sort of divinity in love with Life, all of Life, all its races, its colors, its species, its filth, its odors. Love for me, Promethea. Love what I don't know how to love. Kiss the little boys for me: I would really love to love to love them more than myself, but I can't. Love illiterate souls for me, the way I sincerely desire to love them with an immediate, wise, wordless love, the naked love that is beyond my scope, love them with the strong gentleness of hands that caress wood and stone, because my hands, for such a long time, my hands have been gloved. Kiss everyone for me with love that fits each of their sizes perfectly, with the supple and deft love I do not have, I whose myopia makes me see all people as strangers, all of them different from what I am and surely from what they are, I who, from behind my myopia, astigmatically, carefully, grope with my love, I who prefer not to risk love except in places where they speak my language; love silent people for me the way I regret I am unable to love them, I who am only comfortable in a speaking love; love when you climb up and when you come down, in the Orient and in Asia; love, far from me and you, for me who prefer to love exactly at nose level, I perched in my nest, crinkly eyed, bent over the face of books, I who prefer to let birds and winged creatures come to me so I am sure I have not mistaken their address. Oh, Promethea, you who fly high who fly low who fly far, go, cook for me—I mean: on my behalf—for the people whom I can't just give a good piece of my soul. I only dish myself up, good blood, good food, to a very select number. But you, you dish yourself out equally to the first hundred comers, to me alone, or to all the Indian people. Think about the Mossis tribe in the Upper Volta, think about it in the morning, think about it day after day, think and think until you find a way to go love them with all your energy in reality, think of those I don't think of thinking of, I whose heart's sphere is strictly bounded.

There is room for two Chinas in your soul.

My land is already so full of books that scarcely more than half of Israel would fit in it now.

You are so much more vast than I, my New World. Now, when you travel through certain regions where I had never thought of spending a summer instead of spending it in a book, you make me want to free some of my territories from their ancient inhabitants.

If you see sparks everywhere, Promethea, I think they are the ones made by your hoofs striking even the stickiest rocks and even the most sterile sand.

Promethea's prayer: "My God, make the mist on these eyes that see me as so brilliant never dry up. Preserve this myopia, this astigmatism, make them increase. Make Ash continue to transfigure me. Make her invent me however she pleases, until the end."

—"Amen."

—If you could no longer do your work, what would you do? Promethea asked.

H didn't understand the question.

—If you couldn't. Not teach. Not publish.

—Translate.

—Not that either. If some Moloch demanded a terrible sacrifice.

H wonders.

What would Promethea do if she could no longer invent, create, publish, film? . . . Get a carpenter's license maybe. Could H live without paper, without books? Which is her first love?

What Promethea would like to do: get herself a truck. Sell Chinese soups on the roadside.

Out of love, with love, thanks to love, sell french fries and soda. H tries to imagine the french fries. Looking at her hands. Sees beautiful roads without paper. Tries the soda. Can one write without paper too? If the roads are very, very beautiful.

The hundred and fiftieth day already. And every morning H saw that she loved Promethea and went on:

The sight of the lemon balm all gone to seed upset Promethea so.

Tears brimmed in her lusterless eyes.

The agony of a bad gardener. What did she not do? For life? For flowers? For growth? For the earth? What should she have done?

At the sight of the lemon balm, saw her powerlessness, her smallness, her weakness, saw: the threat of war to children; saw: the beloved woman whom she had not been able to keep from getting sick; saw: everything she had not had time to repair; the house with broken tiles; saw the tree wounded to its heart; saw: America's disappeared abandoned and disappearing in her memory as well.

Saw: everything she had not had the time to see, to love, to save, this year.

Burning with shame felt she was sterile too, gone to seed, dried up. That is why the tears sprang up. As if to remind her that she was moist and alive. "You are a spring."

The sight of Promethea's tears made H desire to wash her feet.

And she loves her also for the sanctity of her need for love. For her terror: "All your life? Do you think so? Do you think you are going to be with me? All your life?"

A sacrilegious thought from H: "Who can say?"

A sacrilegious answer: "Yes, all your life."

Her huge body bent over the little shrub, in the hallway Promethea asks boldly, shyly: Am I the one you love the most?

—The most? (Why would H never be sufficiently boldly shy to ask something so immodest? Because she, H, is only an adult person who has lost that innocent immodesty, the one that does not yet understand the fear of being naked.)

—The most you've ever loved? (That is why Promethea so overjoys her: because she, at least, really wants everything, all, utterly, completely, she wants what she wants and that's All.)

(And H, what does she want? She does want All, but not without fear, without reproach, without blushing.)

188

H did not say: "You're the one I love the most. (Suppose They heard?) You're the one I love.

Because, rather than being in kindergarten where young and greedy and violent truths are spoken, with her backsides comfortably naked, where she would have shown her heart and her genitals to Promethea, she was talking to Promethea in the hallway of a turn-of-the-century house. And it (the house) made her feel how thick her skepticism was. Didn't think they were alone. As if the hallway were her mother. Gazed into Promethea's eyes without speaking: because she wanted to tell the truth. But couldn't tell it, at her age, justly, rightly, and mercifully.

—Nothing compares with how I love you. I don't love you. I don't send love in your direction. I have you, I take you, and I have you. I take you bit by bit. I weigh each morsel and I love it and I like it, and I vow my total love to it. That's how it is. I take it all. I love you in one piece, with one great love that is your equal. Then love divides up into numerous whole loves, able to hold all of my soul.

With a complete and perfect love, I love your neck, I think your neck with my whole being, I contemplate it, I cherish it, I bite it, it is a you. There is nothing of you I do not take, nothing I do not have: the hardest to grasp, a glance bounding out of the cave of your soul, I catch it. There is nothing of you I am willing to leave outside. I take the star spot on your left leg, I take it, I am enriched by it. I collect you with the joy of a diamond merchant: the most ordinary is naturally what is most precious to me. Even all your distraction and forgetfulness, I want them, I am not forgetting them. Your imperfections make me happy.

(I'm not going to tell what they are, for fear she will take them away. Already she has deprived me of the pleasure of finding the toothpaste tube without its top.)

You are the Child whose Business is to get hold of all the love and then to turn herself over completely to loving.

Anyone who loves without counting costs is countlessly

loved. That is something we know: anyone who loves God is divinely loved.

If I don't tell her: "anyone other than me would love you too," it is not solely to avoid getting into a philosophical debate here. It is a thought that I don't want to let her know.

And one day that she loved her even more tenderly, was the day she discovered that Promethea believed in the soul's immortality. And even in the existence of gods. Since H doesn't believe in them at all this pleased her. Because out of love, she preferred that Promethea not have to make herself sad by thinking, as she herself did, about the incredible tragedy of living beings.

—I believe just as absolutely, just as absolutely and vaguely, as the smallest African Pygmy among his trees. I never had any choice.

And it is true. H had already seen, that Promethea, the noble Caucasian mare, had certain expressions on her face—very joyful, very deeply moved by joy—that do not exist in Europe. Had seen this resemblance with the Pygmies when, out of a tremendous gratefulness, they turn whole forests, with their elephants and their snakes, into gods, and you can see it deeply lined in their faces.

—I myself don't believe in God and my belief is as strong and deeply rooted as yours. And what remains of my father? I believe in his absolutely desolate bones; I believe his existence persists as it has moved into my present thought, I believe in the absolute interruption of a life, but also that the marks of a creature who has left time at his time are passed on. I cannot introduce you to my father who does not exist. I cannot introduce you to his innocent bones which make me suffer but do not suffer. I cannot forget such fragile inventions of nature, I forget neither the blood works nor the work of the heart, nor the ultimate resistance of bones, I am in love with the Promethean ambition of bodies, I worship the meticulous immensity of our machines, I worship the pure mystery of the human soul which lives in complete mortality as if all the labor, every work, constructions worthy of gods, were not destined to vanish behind crimson funeral curtains. These are the reasons I adore Promethea like nature herself— because they both are equally mad.

But I cannot forget the curtains coming down. I do not forget the bones, I see Promethea's smile, I see doves on a linden, every day I see the sparkling flecks in her pupils, right up to the last day, I see the last day, I want to see you right up to the end of life on the last day, because afterward I see no more.

Then others see? That's fine. But I, I do not see you. But I have seen you, I have never stopped seeing you. That's fine.

I see the last day.

At the bottom of the pit of despair the well of light that Promethea gave me opens up. Never have I seen a well so deeply, so bright, so limpid. Where does this limpidity come from?

It is the well of Simplicity. It is death that makes everything so simple. Life is otherwise so dark and tortuous.

—Death? I mean: the last day.

At the bottom of the well the thing shining so marvelously, the source of light flooding over all their years, was their death.

They had already had together the finest, most delicate thing, their future death.

—Will you really be willing to die with me someday? one of them asked.

—Yes, hoped the other.

Ever since, they have been swimming their lives in the same shining river, and seeing themselves in the distance, from a distance. They were living ever since death; ever since their last day.

While I am reading this to Promethea she gets nervous and sad, because she thinks she sees a great hole opening up before her hooves. While I am reading, a ladybug no bigger than the pupil of an eye, 25 mm, just as perfect a tiny machine as a miniaturized transistor (and far more charming), with tiny Chinese feet whose delicacy kills you, a red-lacquered back with rows of black sequins stuck at regular intervals on top, lands on the saddening page. She goes about her grooming like this: first, leaning on her right side she cleans the little red feet on her left side for five minutes straight then, without a pause, on her left side rubbing all the little right feet, knees bent, legs stretched out, arms drawn in to her chest.

—Oh! I believe in the ladybug. Is it maybe one of Promethea's gods?

For the whole rest of the day, Ladybug remained serenely on my paper, her legs tucked under, her head on the word "bones," her body scarcely bigger than one of my O's, calmly as a cat. As if she had heard what we were just saying.

I was unable to write that day because of Ladybug: because she was installed on my pile of papers I couldn't reread my last sentences to pick up my train of thought.

I took advantage of it to check the titles of Promethea's Songs of Dawn. I have already forgotten so much! So, I am already rich in forgetting! I get so many presents, I don't have enough arms to embrace my treasures. Why don't I have Ladybug's eight lacquered feet! Am I already drowned in happiness? Is my boat going to turn over?

Here's one: The Song of Baby Moses: it begins like this: "my little boat, my skiff, my pirogue, my willow, my Pharaoh Queen, my Nile, my Ganges, my velvet mud, my river Love," etc. (I like it a lot because it goes around the world by river. But I also like the Song of Houses. And also the one about the Root, that starts like this: dig me up . . . etc. And the one about the Lamb Drunk with Joy who dances for I don't remember whom.)

This morning she woke up in Nepal. Opening her eyes: there were big birds dreaming heavily around us, one all yellow, one all blue, one all red, three big birds each completely one color and not the least spot of another color on them. That was certainly Nepal. I was able to start again:

Something H secretly loved was how Promethea did not know all the things she gave her, did not know and was worried, did not know how she gave her and was desperately unhappy about it, thought she gave her nothing, because up until now she had not had the chance or the time to give what she would have liked to give her, so she trembled with sorrow, her chest was heaving, just like in the story of the bird prince shut up in a cage who would like to give the sky and its boundless realms to the maiden he loves, and in his agonies he sings of everything he would give if the cage gave way, and he sings so sweetly that the maiden feels herself in raptures, her body redolent with sweetness, and the bird doesn't know it, the bird suffers so much that he does not hear the bars of the cage return his strains with the sweetest of music, he weeps and does not notice the beauty that his small voice awakens all over the room, the maiden would like to tell him, but she is so beside herself, this pain is so beautiful, she would like to reassure him, but she is so intoxicated, she is afraid, if she does not persuade the bird that he is giving her unheard of joy that she will have to open the cage and set him free, to lose him, but she would like to soothe him, but she is struck dumb with pleasure, but she would like to tell him: your desire to give me all is so great that it gives me more than all, but happily, her ecstasy is such that she is unable to murmur a single word. . . .

(Today was the hundred and sixtieth day, nothing happened. They both lived all this nothing with a keen, keen, keen, miraculously keen, joy. Is that happiness, that nothing peacefully going by, white and motionless like the seagull who went down the river this morning, seated tranquilly on his greenwater chariot? Like Ladybug on my train of thought?)

is unable to murmur:

. . . you are giving me all that you desire to give me, and more than that, everything you have not thought of desiring, you who do not know that it is the desire to give that gives. You give me all the furs that you would like to madly splurge choosing you give me rivers of white fur, you give me all the streets of Kyoto with their temples and arcades,

you give me a certain golden cloth to be found nowhere in the world except one shop in Cairo where Bedreddin left it a very, very long time ago. How you found it after so many centuries is an incredible story, but I am keeping it for another day. You give me an orchard where the trees that make you dream are in bloom, you give me, if only you could, the sultan of Damas's purse, and in your desire I am wearing the pure splendor of jewels liberated from their haggling destiny. You give me the rarest of laughing music for which I would have sold all my books, and you return all my books to me with the music, and with their melodies a palace where they can resound, the white horse to race with joy to the Ganges, and the elephant to come back and hear the concert's eternal suite. Also the breadth of the Ganges, all its gold, all its forces. And also dreams of trips and their trips in all the countries where we will go some day or we will never go, never again. And also Afghanistans and in the midst of pearly mountains and in the midst of green and red wars and under fire you slip into my mouth a piece of peace full of magical sesames. Oh, you give me mercies and brother-hoods, and arks of memories for today, and the fleet of frail emergency arks floating over wars to Survivals, sometimes never getting there, sometimes sinking, sometimes going aground, but not without having first tried everything. You give me tries and their various luck.

You give me everything I want from this point on. All the hardships I have had, all the happiness I have not had and all the happiness I have had, everything I have lived, this is what you give me, and this is today, and what was fine and what was bad is so fine, and everything I have not had has now been turned into gold and given to me, oh my treasure house of things not had is immense, my casket contains marvelous mishaps. How happy I am to have been sometimes so sad, what joy I have now when you give me back these sadnesses wrapped up in transparent papers of remembrance, I see them shining through the silk, present now, and it is an unheard of wealth, I would have liked to have been even unhappier. But I don't have much to complain of. My agonies have been rare and my losses exceptional. Today I am able to take joy in having known the fire of a mother's tears, those tears that eat one's eyes alive; anyone who has not lived through her child's dying will never feel their bite in her eyes; I have fine abandonments to celebrate, I know a lot about misadventures, praise be Misfortune today, like so many other women I have had my Birenes, from Olympia to my friend, my sister, the Portuguese concierge at our apartment building (but she, grieving, is unable even to write the letters that brought relief to the nun in her passion), I cried out, weeping to someone who did not come alas did not come never came, praise be unto thee Great Divine Wheel, you who overwhelm us with pain and blindness, who torment and terrify us and promise no end to the torture, and drive us into the night toward infernal world weariness, you who smile tenderly and say nothing, but we, our eyes eaten away by salt, do not see you smile, we shiver as we make our way and we never even guess what a good fire you are fixing for us, you who grant us the favor of putting our hearts on the rack,

How happy I am that I believed at first that my life would travel without mishap along youth's High Plateaus, where the graceful fauns who modeled for poets take flight, that I was suddenly utterly let down, that I lost this head in a plague that plunged one whole long year of my reality into a shadowy nightmare, that I was stricken with malevolent plagues as if I were Egypt, when I thought that among my race I was the one safely sheltered, that I lost my second reason on the second throw of the dice, that I had to make up my mind to go down the angels' ladder to resignation, that I was happy not to be unhappy, that three times I thought I saw the future turning toward me with a smile, that I ran toward it three times, my heart full of praises, and that, three times just at the instant I touched it I saw its beautiful face contort, twisted in rage. Blessed be each trust I had that was stabbed to death, the destruction of every naive faith, the severed hands of love. Blessed be my completely ordinary fate. I was used to it. Blessed (after the violence of pain) be the springtime of tame pain.

I am standing here, in the midst of my quivering and laughing life, shouting like the Other, "I want to be queen," and in fact all morning long she is the queen, and the morning lasts until the last accounting of our days, I look back, pressed against the window of your heart, I look at my past lives over there, my burning life, my life of ashes, my frozen life, I look at them with new eyes, quivering also, I see, I rejoice, I rule, the kingdoms of my pain make my kingdoms of joy even richer, my coffers abundant in all realities.

I want what I have had, I want what I will have: I want to be royally human, I want to cry some more, I want troubles, discouragements, dreaded ordeals, whatever I don't want, I want it too—even sicknesses?—I don't want to say no, I want to flee nothing, I want to live you through fatigue, money problems, the stupid mountains that overwhelm us when we wake up as moles, I want to live you here and now Promethea, today, with no glory, with all its ruts and exhaustion, but today, with our heavy legs, I would go to the stars even if spurs are necessary. I who tumbled down the ladder and broke something in my ability to live the paltry life of dreams—a life not without its charms but lacking flesh and warmth and seasons, a life with nothing worth dying for, and I went along softly dreaming, my head resting on a stone, with the desert for my world and books for stars, I who lived amidst the ghosts of consolations, not moving for fear of tearing the stars in my spider's tent, I who lived in despair's flimsy comfort, and now I can congratulate myself for having been so unsullied by any hope and then to have been at the mercy of the most violent mercy.

And now all I want are the ups and downs of reality, I want to live these days, I want to take pleasure in the greatest and the middling and everyday difficulties and defeat them, or together not defeat them,

—you give me daily royalty, Promethea, the royalty one must conquer every morning and defend everyday, let's be queens a hundred times and if we are defeated let's be royally defeated, since finally we are in the real world, the surprising, insane, torn, faltering, world in crisis, the unfair, tumultuous, threatening, modern, polluting, knowing, egotistical one, the ram, the astrakhans, the butcher and the wheat, the monster, the doctor, the world with a bull's horns and hedgehog's belly, the world of Lebanons, of napalms, of palm gardens, of massacred daughters, of very nasty peoples and very sweet ones, the world of undying hatreds, of dragons transformed into the chiefs of very big States, the toiling world, of shoes and finances, the two-faced two-sexed world, the true, the elegant, the inventor of eloquent perfumes and of huge apartment buildings as beautiful as grasshoppers, the inconsiderate, cruddy, intoxicating, spineless, dreamer of planets, rival of stars, equal of mass graves,

since you lifted the crimson curtains on mad cities, the noble and the whoring cities, anthill nations and distraught races, I want to come from everywhere with you, I want to discover our century's poles, I who soaked my days in the temperate springs around the middle of the world, halfway between death and life, middling out my existence, now you give me the sharp taste of this century still only a thousand years old in the bitter steppes down below, where it is unhoped-for luck to be born a buffalo rather than a person, but in certain blond countries at the top of the world it is already on its way swiftly humming down its narrow celestial paths, into its three thousandth year with its trusting eyes, its virgin eyes, with its modern teeth guaranteed to sparkle, and the green sculptured steel calves of its legs, with its very young, very flighty memories, with well-thought-out projects that are entirely feasible next year, with electronic eroticism, you provide me with the courage to look at this doubly ignorant century—the ancient hunchbacked ignorance whose face sees its only heaven in the meager earth, and the new ignorance, proud of itself—and with the courage to go all over this earth, lovingly detesting it and hating it out of love. I take the world that grows younger as it grows old and the world that turns back into mud as it is born: without you to love them beyond my own fury and compassion I would stay away from them like poison. I who survived snuggled in the Book I made myself in the hollow of the Tree of Knowledge. And flat on my belly over a poem, before my eyes a garden closed off by a pure mountain created on the model of a Japanese woodprint, I no longer wanted to go back down, I did not want to go back into my book, my heart fallen, my tongue bitten in anger again, one more soul torn by the brambles and my pretty shoes burning my feet as if I had really walked on beggars' hands; I preferred not to be born anymore, it was too hard, that first misery in the street killed me, I would have killed at the first look of scorn. I, with my little misfortunes, my little hands and my big dreams, I no longer had the strength to bear the weight of the world's unhappiness.

But with you, Promethea, I am ready and willing to leap out of the Book, even to go visit some emaciated people, even if I don't forget all my beautiful shoes, each of which is worth more than a bag of rice, even if my closet full of satins and of lace shirts weighs suddenly on my soul like a ton of rice, despite my papers, my silks, my priceless treasures of phrases, rhythms, daydreams, with you I will go down whatever streets you want, barefoot you redeeming my beautiful shoes, but this is not something you do on purpose, barefoot you,

you imagine me (if you could manage it) in swanskin slippers, I who see myself hopping befeathered in your great white footprints, you who if you could would voluptuously, graciously, buy me such beautiful shoes worth at least ten rare volumes and a bag of flour and your only regret is not being able to carry away the whole shop, yes I want to go with you, and without looking at myself anymore, even into a cage of refugees clutching the wire fence over two ditches at the frontier, I unmasked, but you with the same open face whether in the South or in the North,

I'll go, once my little personal hesitations are overcome, I promise, because you believe very strongly that one can change things a bit, and even if I don't believe it, you believe so strongly, much more strongly than I, you give me the ultimate hope, Promethea, you give me the hope that is still fresh and new but cherished so, already because of you I hope I am wrong, I am praying that you win out over me, Promethea, already I am a willing captive of your faith as I perform my lack of faith, and just as I am, Infidel and uncertain and myopic as they come, even if I do not yet or ever believe, I will joyfully go beyond myself, my wishes go with you and too bad for my ideas, I pray for your Victory:

dear God, or whatever singular or plural power you are, who determine the fate of human beings, you the peoples, you the laws, you the weapons, you the ideas of good and evil, you the luck or calculations, whoever you are, you the fighters, you the philosophies, you the forces of society, etc., make this woman, Promethea, be gloriously right, make her crush me and confound my sincere faithlessness

this is the so fragile but so fervent hope which I'll bring when I go with you, Promethea, into the countries where we will be afraid and into the countries where we will be ashamed. It will be the same fear, but not the same shame—I know because the other day when the Polish woman cried out "come even if you don't have any money or any medicine or anything to eat, that isn't important, just come and talk to us," afterward Promethea burst into tears, in the street crammed so full of things and crammed so full of people who were buying and not talking and eating without talking, and who did not embrace each other, and I held Promethea in my arms, and I was not crying, I was not crying (because I saw myself going in and out of my Book the way you would go in and out of a fancy shop, never coming down from my dream. Am I hard on myself? The way one should be: a gesture of friendship. The truth is that when things are disturbing I always make myself desired a little. My Book in the tree was so comfortably set up that often I forgot it was a cage).

So I did not cry but that was fine. I was sad and happy because it was Promethea's right to shed all the tears of shame, I was proud of this shame. I would have liked to cry too, but I do not have what it takes to be proud enough not to blush over having such intense and generous attacks of shame. I kept my shame dry once more. Promethea trembled with her whole body because she felt she could not do everything—which she calls "doing nothing"—drenched in sweat, like the mare who finds she is trapped in a bird cage.

For the love of these tears and these sweats I'll go, I'll go tomorrow or I'll go as soon as I finish transcribing these notebooks, I'll go I'm sure, even if it is unenthusiastically and egotistically,

Because things purely not possible for me are the purest of possibility for you—I'll go because you don't ask me to, because when you keep on looking back as you gallop off to Asia you are asking me to—I'll go out of love where I don't feel virtuous enough to go out of "solidarity," not humble enough, not confident enough—

—Not confident enough in whom?

—I don't really know. In humanity. In history? Who knows, in myself maybe.

—But it is true that I have confidence in Promethea.

—Does that mean you have confidence in humanity without knowing it?

—If Promethea is humanity. But she isn't.

—But she is part of it.

—But yesterday when I said to Promethea: "I have confidence in you"—because this is such a pure truth that I love to say it—she shivered. For that very thing. Because she is afraid that my confidence will be disappointed. She wept: "I want to do everything well for you but I'm so afraid I won't succeed." Promethea, for this fear, for these tears, I bless you.

—"If you had no confidence in me I wouldn't be afraid. You give me something so wonderful. I'm afraid I don't deserve it."

—What I am giving you is nothing that belongs to me, Promethea. It is just yourself, you running through me throwing off sparks, your eyes blazing with fear, blazing with hope, I am giving you your own fire. All I do is breathe very gently on your night embers and handfuls of stars fly out.

I bless you, Promethea, you who want to do things right so you will be loved. How could you disappoint my confidence in you, you who fear with all your soul for it? You who love my confidence like your very own daughter?

—And what if the dish of beef with seven herbs I made for tonight isn't any good? It smells like it stuck to the pan.

—I won't be (wouldn't be) disappointed. I will (would) eat your worry too.

—And what if, when I finish the house, you see that it isn't beautiful, not its shape, not its color?

—I have confidence in your hands, Promethea, and in your dreams. If it's awful I love you, and if it's beautiful I love you too.

I bless you, Promethea, you who want to be deserving, you who believe you have to fight for the love of love. What different fervent roads did you take to escape the Christian epics you never read? Your neck drenched, your powerful heart chanting in your breast, across forty generations, you who were conceived in a romance sometime around 1160, you who come from the farthest reaches of the earth, from what east or west come the splendid dreams breathing inspirations whose secret our times have lost into your works, from what civilizations filled with wonder at being human do you descend upon our bored cities, your eyes streaming with promising visions, your blood raging with passion for the world's inhabitants, you who think we all, we who are born from miracles of matter, we all are the lucky starters in the Marvelous Race, the beneficiaries of this vast luck, Life.

How fresh and medieval your soul is, you who pierce our dreary bottled-up desires with the stubbornness of an arrow shot from the Golden Bow, you who believe that the earthly paradise is not lost, that we have been given it right here, in bad shape, eaten by populations that are too fat and gnawed at by peoples that are too thin, and covered with excrement and hideous monuments, and that we, each person and in groups, have to free it, save it, restore it, and since there is such a gigantic amount of work to be done, you go to it without wasting a day, you who think that every human being is given, in exchange for her birth, the mission of protecting the world's beauty, and of leaving the world clean and wiser when she leaves.

You, who some Mondays head fervently out into the world, like three young knaves determined to build a temple, kill a dragon, save a battered woman, some Wednesdays armed with spears and swords that conquer without wounding, you head out into foreign camps like two women capable of leading coed troops without humiliating a single man, off you go afraid, into the greatest of dangers, to try and free people who are the captives of horribly modernized forms of primitive tyranny. And other days you have fun like five children who play at possessing every happiness in life, you want to be happy and you are showered with happiness, you want unheard of caresses and your wishes come true, you want candies, presents, exotic fruits, apartments wrought as finely as jewels, and you get all the things grownups are not imaginative enough to ask for.

What virgin peaks have you crossed over, I wonder, what sunbathed heights, to get here so young and urgent and tireless in this gray time which, having retired from grace intends to sit in front of the television for all eternity, using its stiff joints and its good sense for an excuse to be cushioned alive? How did you get such faithful eyes? You, at least, have never lost sight of the heavenly face of Life awaiting us at the end of our race, seeming often so sad and rarely lit up with joy the way she would like to be. Awaits us to remind us, on the last day, what it is up to us to bring along from the other side. And so often we only have a few days left, sometimes only the last one. But sometimes, we pass on with hearts full of all the days we did not forget to devote to Life.

You, Promethea, who are always wondering if you haven't failed to fulfill your promises, if you haven't disappointed Life today, if you did not give her a big enough present, one fine enough, I can predict that you will have vast riches to put on your boat, on the last day. You, who have lived almost every day. But, for myself, I know that if tomorrow is my last day I will not have even half my existence to carry with me.

—Promise me that you will always tremble, Promethea. If you didn't tremble anymore I wouldn't love you anymore.

—Why?

Promethea doesn't know that maybe H started loving to see her tremble the day of the demonstration for Argentina. Didn't she tell her? H didn't know either. But that was the day she came unexpectedly upon Promethea's soul in naked prostration before her fellow creatures as if before her own gods. Discreetly H pretended to have seen nothing, but Promethea's soul had already been taken into hers. A soul as moving as Bedreddin Hassan's extraordinary white bosom when he was found asleep in his dark blue underwear at the gates of Damascus, so naked and so sweet that the village people adopted him, without knowing why. Me too.

Promethea does not have the sort of soul that is in fashion: it weeps, it shivers, it trembles, really, the way it hasn't been done in Europe for almost two centuries. This is because her only fashion is the soul's.

—And what if the suit I designed for you in Balsaran silk is cut too small, what if it's too snug, what if the silk itself turns against me and the dress is always wrinkled?

—Make love so that I can console you soon.

—And the crystal bird I took from its nest in an old Bohemian glassworks for you, I told you it looked like you, and now here it is in crystal bits in the bottom of my bag?

—I could have broken it myself. Then what despair!

—And what if I forget the time we are supposed to meet today, while you are working so hard to write me down to the tenth of a second, and what if I come looking for you a long, long time afterward? Won't you lose confidence?

—I prefer that you not forget, please. But if you do forget, I swear that a little later, when the storm panicking my thoughts like swallows is over, I will really forget that you forgot.

I am no champion of love. I was not born in 1160. I did not grow up among the Lightfoot Tribe. I did not live for a year in an Afghan tent. I was not raised among sheep in a beautiful meadow by the caresses of a shepherdess. When I was saying my first words, my soul was not cut from the moist cloth of a river.

I am no saint at all: one is born a saint. One is a saint without knowing it. Would I say that Promethea is a saint? She was born with a kind of wild saintliness, but it is not her profession. Her real profession is to deliver orphan temples from the serpent trees devouring them and innocent sculptured stone goddesses shot at by armies, whose breasts men who have turned back into monsters destroy with hand grenades; and all the while she is building more mobile temples, inventing flying Angkors. I just tell stories: She engineers the Dream.

—But all I'm trying to say really is: I just love you, Promethea. The love I have for you is the best kind: it is raised on my body and will last as long. It is the truest thing I can create: yes, it is entirely handmade, with as much blood as you like. But it is just me loving you. I, with my worked-over soul, started all over a thousand times, retouched, my much-improved soul these past few years. But not saintly, not serene. Just athletic and in good shape. But I am no Indian brave. I am just a nervous white kid, a stubborn girl, whose free desires are too big for her, who wanted one day to become a great lady. A woman big enough not to have to ask anyone and to catch this strange royal doll passing in front of her wild smallness, passing her by, too high and too expensive for a little girl, too calm and smiling and plump for me to bear not getting it—then a tiny bit of heart was consumed. From rage, for the golden eyes of a forbidden Woman, I grew up. It was not sweet love that made me grow up. I grew on jealous love, Arab love, gritting my teeth for a forbidden Moorish woman. I am not a spontaneous heroine. What is more, I am not a heroine at all: I never really freed any people or any tomb. I have not conquered plains or crowns. I never had the least idea of conquering Promethea. And yet I saw her running for ten springtimes in the prairie flowing at the foot of my Book Tree. And through my leaves I loved her, from the top of my Book, beyond my desire, beyond time, roaming her life in some other story that I was not writing, that I read peacefully, my heart withdrawn into a flying story, far from streets, far from prairies, far from the whims of reality. And then? Next: in another story, after ten years, the doll Lady of Beauty comes back and stops of her own will in front of the house of the one no longer thinking of her, and she comes in, and she asks for something to drink. And next: at the end of ten years, a day of deluge, Promethea suddenly came in through the window, her mane streaming with bitter waters. And then? I rubbed her down and dried her. Meanwhile everything in the kitchen burned. And then? The flood kept coming. The next day everything burned again. When I tried to put the fire out I burned my writing hand. And next. The flood lasted forty days. Until, in the end, the same sort of thing having happened to just about everything, at the instant that the rain stopped, when I thought: "now she can go back to her prairie, it's time," at that very instant a spark fell on my heart, and vroom! my entire Book up in smoke, flames as high as this pouring from my breast, I thought "me too, it's time, into the prairie."

—Do I deserve you, Promethea? I never even ask myself? Why? I don't know if I know how to deserve. I know how to: do well on exams; desire, admire, without coveting; sing. That's all. Deserving is a medieval art. I do have a mystical soul for talking to other people or for my favorite characters. But I always use a more contemporary soul for myself, one informed about the progress made in physics and psychoanalysis, one proudly and humbly aiming within limited probabilities of victory.

. . . . .

————Here Promethea interrupted me with violent protests. She shouted:

—That's not true! Oh no! That's not true.

—Yes, it is.

—That's wrong, absolutely wrong.

—That's not true. I mean, no, it's not wrong.

—Yes, yes, it's wrong. You aren't fair to yourself. Besides everyone will be able to see you are not telling the truth. Because if H is the way you say she is, she couldn't talk about Promethea the way she does.

That is not true at all. Promethea does not know that a finite being may see something of the infinite, etc. Obviously, I see what she means: "If you love me being great, it's because there is some greatness in you, etc. You are the one speaking, so you are also speaking about yourself, etc. How would you know the twelfth century if you weren't from it? etc." That is not entirely wrong, but it is thoroughly debatable.

And by the way, there was no debating. Because Promethea made me swear to record her protest. Hereby recorded.

—It's my book after all, isn't it?

—That's absolutely true.

Promethea would like everything to be true in this book. I mean: everything that is in this book to be true outside of this book. She's a dreamer! All I can promise her is that everything in this book is true. I live it. I see it. Maybe I also dream it? But at least, as far as Promethea is concerned I dream the truth. Even if I woke up I would see her the way I see her. I wrote Promethea in our language. But she would not lose anything even in translation. I am ready to defend my Promethea in any language at all. Which is, moreover, something that frightens her. But she too loves my Promethea and would like to have the strength to prove me right. As for all the rest I am ready to take on any objections.

—I left off with . . . "of victory" . . . To return:

Or is it being lucky that makes me deserving? I am thrilled with joy to have gotten something I do not deserve. Or is joy the only thing that makes me deserving?

—I don't deserve you, Promethea

I never wanted you.

I never hoped for you.

You were awarded to me.

Just as if you were owed me

You were not owed me

As if you were owed me,

Absolutely unafraid

I took you

Unafraid and joyful

Because you were not owed me.

Maybe for a moment I deserved you: because the joy with which I took what was not owed me was so pure. Out of egotism. By virtue of my egotism. For just a moment, without wanting to, I must have deserved you: through the magnitude and purity of my egotism. When magically you were sent to me through the window and immediately I was magically sure you were for me. How I laughed! I bragged about my happiness all over the country. Because I did not deserve it. I had my day of saintliness: when a grownup's egotism becomes as huge and radiant as a child's, it's saintliness.

—And now that you have me?

—Because I have you I can want you, I want you. But I don't want to deserve you by myself: I would not know how to do it with a true heart. My heart is not transparent like yours. I want you to be given to me always like the first grace. If I deserved you myself I would no longer deserve you. I want something better than me for you. Anything better to offer you I have to find where you are. Because the world stretching out before your prairie is far vaster, more populous, more diverse and still unknown than the one I set up to keep in my garden.

—But then why can I want to deserve you?

—You have vast virgin spaces in front of you. But I see my frontiers already. You have the thousand years before you that I have behind me. It is time for me to begin to grow younger. I don't want to go at the speed of this century's flattening light. I want to derail. I want to return ahead, much later, long, long ago, where you grew up, Promethea. I want to go back among the savages, I want to join the tribe of the Headstrong again, the ones who refused to learn to be careful, or to ridicule generosity, or the laws devaluing personal courage.

When I am a thousand years younger, that is if we turn west a thousand more years, if I circle the world galloping on the magic Mare, then I will love you more amply.

—I would like so much to be as beautiful as this Promethea you are making up. (Says Promethea.)

—I'm not making her up. I'm only making a fair copy of the truth. The Beautiful cannot be made up. It is discovered or it is not seen at all. I am looking at you. I am just looking at you.

The author of what I describe is not myself, it is the Other. First of all it is you, it is the woman, it is the queen, it is the

Child, it is a person who is greater than I and who surpasses you as well, whom you do not know. I am your scribe. Without false modesty, I expect there are many people who will recognize you and praise the faithfulness of my method.

It is like the love I have for you: so much bigger than myself. I struggle not to be false to it, to broaden myself so I won't smother inside my narrow rib cage. And sometimes love reaches my limits, I am incapable of more, and it flies over me with the roar of wings.

Does that mean that it is not I who love you, Promethea? I don't know who loves you, but everything loving you is me.

Yes, me, the one who tore herself from my ground with a huge burst of fire to love you. I am the one who burns and carries me far beyond myself. I and the Other too. It is not just me, it is God passing through me to run with you.

And now: I'm afraid. How happy I am to feel such beautiful fear at last!

Because to cry for joy one needs to die of fear.

You have given death back to me, you who give yourself to death, you give me everything to death. All, completely. So I must thank someone because of you.

Promethea, whom do you want me to thank?

Today is the last day for Promethea's book. Last night I couldn't sleep, I read the story of Bedreddin Hassan until the sun came up. Bedreddin Hassan did not have a peaceful night either: he kept waking up and wondering whether he was dreaming or awake. Did not trust his happiness. Me too. Trying to make sure it was there, ran my eyes all around the room. It really was the room. Contemplated then, at length, Promethea's face. It really was her. And she had not slept peacefully either.

She wondered if what had snatched her suddenly from sleep was the thought of the last day or the thought of the new opening day. Throughout the morning then, each one had her turn at being first anxious then brave. When one had tears in her eyes, the other quickly told her what the sailboat for the next trip was going to be like.

I said: It's not the book that's ending. It's a new life beginning.

Yes. . . . But then around noon I am the one upset. Until Promethea makes up the song of consolations.

So I am recording it here because it still belongs to this book:

—"I'd like to give you raisin cookies, candies, golden chains, silver bells, loops of barley sugar, pomegranites, almonds, pistachios, little bikes, golden sugar cubes, . . ."

—More, more!

"———little paper dragons, crimson satin ribbons, two Moorish dolls with clothes to dress them, sheets of jasmined silk, little pearl-embroidered slippers, scarves like birds, oranges, dates you would die for, thousands of songs with silver spangles, and . . ."

Promethea kept stringing irresistible dreams on her magic string. She made me a necklace that was really soothing.

That is why I would like Promethea's book to "end" here, like that: everyone can try on the necklace; and you can add all the things you would really like to receive.

Promethea wonders if it's possible just to "finish like that."

—It's all up to *you* now.

But afterward I was worried again about the book's name.

—Don't you want to call it *Promethea Unbound*? Promethea was surprised.

—I go back and forth. It's good. But there's too much in it. It's too full of other people's tears and other histories.

So they started to play What-If-We-Called-It. Promethea went first:

What if we called it: Promethea Disappeared.

H shuddered: No.

—Promethea in Russia? Promethea has Problems. Promethea in a Balloon. Promethea in the Theater.

—Promethea's Youth.

Promethea said: wrong style. H leaned toward Goethe and Promethea more toward Becassine. They made each other laugh. Kept at it: Promethea in China. —Promethea's Vacation. —No: Promethea on Vacation. Promethea among the Pygmies. Promethea the Secret Agent. Promethea the Doctor. Promethea gets Married. —The Sufferings of Promethea. —No: Promethea the Grandmother. —No, my turn! Promethea at the Police Station. —Promethea Reads the Bible. —No! That was meant to be funny. —Promethea Moves Out. Promethea Opens a Restaurant. No, no.

Promethea won. Yes, Promethea was the one who won, she thought of twenty titles in a row without trying. Whereas H found hardly any; and moreover kept saying: no, no, no, stop! and laughing. But she was also a little angry. And a little confused: because really Promethea had brilliantly carried off the last page. I insist on saying that here. But H was the one who thought of Promethea is Being Silly.

—So is that where we stop? (H is the one who wants to stop.)

—Yes. (But Promethea is still running.)

—Thank you.

But Promethea runs on:

—Ah I forgot! Promethea Falls in Love.

—Falls?

—Is.

In the European Women Writers series